"The perfect guide for the boardroom. With so much information available online, it's hard to know where to begin when you begin acting in office. How to Avoid a Fall from Grace *cuts through the legal jargon and explains directors' duties in a way that is relevant to senior executives. A must-read for any leader interested in success."*

—**Bruce Griffiths** OAM, director, *Quickstep Holdings Ltd*
and director, *Carbon Revolution Pty Ltd*

"It's rare to find a book on this topic that is both comprehensive and readable. How to Avoid a Fall from Grace *manages it effortlessly, combining technical excellence with practicality and accessibility in one very helpful read."*

—**Michael Iwaniw,** chairman,
Select Harvests Ltd

"As the chair of a not-for-profit organisation I find timely, relevant, and easily accessible assistance is imperative, and this book provides just that. It guides you through the relevant legislation and other legal concerns with pithy and relatable examples that show, not just tell, what you should be doing."

—**Bill Griffiths**, chairman,
Carrington Cottages Management Incorporated

"A shortcut/roadmap to success—let Sarah guide you through the corporate maze."

—**Malcolm Jackman,** chairman,
SubZero Group Ltd, and chief executive,
South Australian Fire & Emergency Commission

"*This book is an indispensable resource; informative and practical, it covers almost every eventuality a director will have to deal with. It is a must for any leader's bookshelf.*"

—**Aaron LeCornu,** director, *Kornblum Pty Ltd*

"How to Avoid a Fall from Grace *takes the often complex legal challenges that every director faces and provides answers and solutions that are truly accessible. The material is engaging and the examples relevant. It is an excellent reference guide for directors.*"

—**Alicia Burgemeister,** senior in-house lawyer

"*In easy-to-understand, straightforward language,* How to Avoid a Fall From Grace *provides a comprehensive overview of the key information directors need to know. Canvassing topics such as directors' duties, financial reporting obligations, and personal liability, this informative and relevant resource is one that I expect readers will return to often.*"

—**Rachel Humphrys,** compliance manager, *Deloitte Australia*

"*A pocket legal expert.* How to Avoid a Fall from Grace *is a handy reference book—easy to read and full of real-life examples many leaders can relate to.*"

—**Mark De Wit,** chief executive officer, *Futuris Automotive Group*

"*A 'one of its kind' book—if only* How to Avoid a Fall From Grace *existed 20 years' ago! It is a practical text which is perfect, particularly useful for busy Executives. I have searched high and low – there is no comparable resource to* How to Avoid a Fall From Grace.*"

—**David Marino**, managing director and chief executive officer, *Quickstep Holdings Ltd*

"Starting and building a business can be a complex and daunting process, especially for those doing so for the first time. While it's completely normal to feel overwhelmed by the sheer number of legal and administrative issues that must be dealt with, fortunately there are now incredible resources available for entrepreneurs to access.

In How to Avoid a Fall From Grace, *Sarah Bartholomeusz has compiled an approachable, but very complete, reference for directors seeking to better understand the responsibilities, risks, and obligations that come with serving on the board of a company.*

Whether a seasoned director or first-board novice, I highly recommend directors and "future directors" read, consult, and refer back to How to Avoid a Fall From Grace *as a tremendously helpful tool in their business arsenal."*

—**David McLauchlan,** chairman and chief executive officer,
Buddy Platform, Inc.

How to Avoid a

FALL *from*

GRACE

How to Avoid a

FALL *from*

GRACE

Legal Lessons for Directors

SARAH BARTHOLOMEUSZ

Project management and text design by Michael Hanrahan Publishing
Cartoon images by Daniel Corcoran, Characteristix
Cover design by Peter Reardon

Disclaimer
The material in this publication is of the nature of general comment only, and does not represent professional advice. It is not intended to provide specific guidance for particular circumstances and it should not be relied on as the basis for any decision to take action or not take action on any matter which it covers. Readers should obtain professional advice where appropriate, before making any such decision. To the maximum extent permitted by law, the author and publisher disclaim all responsibility and liability to any person, arising directly or indirectly from any person taking or not taking action based on the information in this publication.

TO MY PARENTS
Thank you for my love of books and lessons.

TO MY HUSBAND
Thank you for teaching me that not
all lessons come from books.

Darwin Cula

Camilla Jeffries

Ruth Barker

Kasia Jaruleska

Jessica Lucas

David Chuter

Thank you

Lisa Jane C Miedes

Daniel Corcoran ——————— ——————— Melissa Jones

Darya Kraynaya

Daniela Cecere-Palazzo

Greg Marsh

Sheena Jackson

David Bartholomeusz

Daniella Loyovich

Advantage Family!

FOREWORD

Following an executive career, I have been a director of my own business for over a decade, and I have witnessed and experienced many of the challenges Australian company directors face every day.

Being a company director is complex, and with the fast pace of the modern work environment, we often find ourselves overstretched and time poor. Taking time out to read this practical and insightful guide for company directors is a wise investment of your precious time.

How to Avoid a Fall from Grace provides you the warning signs to know when to stop what you are doing and ask for advice—before it's too late. Sarah offers years of legal experience and makes the topics approachable by using real-life case studies so we can identify our own red flags as we venture into risky, rewarding territory.

The ongoing challenge we all face is that laws are complex and ever changing. This book will carefully guide you through both state and federal obligations on your directorship. Sarah also introduces the myriad of government agencies that you will have to liaise with, from the Australian Taxation Office to state environmental agencies. The book also explains the case law that directly pertains to the duties and conduct of a director.

Although this book might not unlock the innermost secrets to being a successful director, it *will* teach you how to protect your most valuable asset—your reputation. You'll learn how to use the responsibility that comes with being a director correctly and effectively and enjoy greater peace of mind as you go about your day-to-day duties along your road to success.

Kelly Jamieson
Managing Director
The Edible Blooms Group

TABLE OF CONTENTS

INTRODUCTION

My name is Sarah Bartholomeusz, and I am the founder of You Legal. I have been a corporate and commercial lawyer for over 12 years and have also acted as in-house counsel for a number of leading Australian companies. You Legal belongs to a dynamic and innovative new category of law firm that provides flexible legal services to companies. At You Legal we provide leaders in growing companies with the confidence and certainty they need to make bold decisions.

Throughout my career, I have often been surprised that people are not fully aware of the circumstances in which they may be personally exposed when they are acting as a director or officer of a company. It is important to remember that being a director of any company comes with certain obligations and may even give rise to personal liability for decisions made while undertaking this role. In order to feel empowered, leaders must fully understand their risk profile.

My concern encouraged me to work closely with clients to help them understand their obligations. In order to help our clients and their teams understand the risk profiles of their organisations, I created a comprehensive 'Legal Lessons'. This allowed our clients, many being entrepreneurs, family-owned businesses, and ASX-listed companies, to become aware of the risks in their business. They are then able to confidently prepare for the future. The popularity of the 'Legal Lessons' with our clients encouraged me to write this book. I hope you will find it valuable.

This is the inevitable legal disclaimer (you would have been disappointed if it were not here): This book is an overview of the law at a specific point in time and is very general in nature. It should not be relied on as a substitute for legal advice. In addition, with the law in this area changing regularly, this book is unlikely to remain a comprehensive guide for long. But we hope that it can be used as a guide to mitigate your personal risk and highlight some items worthy of consideration and discussion in the boardroom. Please feel free to contact us regarding anything in this book, and we may be able to assist you.

The leading piece of law that governs directors' duties is the *Corporations Act 2001* (Cth). We'll refer to it as the Act for simplicity. The parenthetical abbreviation (Cth), which stands for the jurisdiction of the Commonwealth, is placed next to the name of the legislation to indicate that this is a federal piece of legislation and applies at the national level.

At the moment, you might feel as if you are travelling through the corporate jungle in the dark. This book aims to help by turning on the light so you can see what you don't know that you should know. When that light is turned on, you will be able to see all the crocodiles in the jungle. You may not find that comforting, but at least you will know that they are out there and how to spot them.

CHAPTER 1

Directors' 101

B efore you even utter the word *director* when talking about your job, it is essential to understand the Act. It includes important legal definitions and terms you need to fully understand your legal obligations. These terms include *director, senior manager,* and *officer.* The Act imposes requirements on each of these categories of individuals.

What exactly is the Act? In short, it is the principal legislation that regulates companies in Australia. If you really want to get detailed, you could read all five volumes and ten chapters that comprise the Act. Or I can just give you a brief overview:

WHO ARE THESE PEOPLE?

The Act refers to *officers* of the corporation. This can mean many things, including:

- **A company director.** This includes both executive and non-executive officers.

- **A company secretary.** This is mandatory for public companies. A company secretary has several important duties, including signing contracts, supervising and managing board policies and procedures, and keeping diligent and accurate minutes during meetings.

- **Any significant decision maker.** This is a person who participates in making substantial or significant decisions for the company.

- **Employees of the company.** In the context of directors' duties under the Act, the term *employees* refers to senior managers who are involved in decision making for the company. It normally does not mean all of the company employees; this would be quite rare. However, keep in mind there may be other legislation in place that imposes obligations on employees within specific industries, organisations, or areas of responsibility.

WHAT'S YOUR TYPE?

There are different types of directors. It all depends on the level of involvement they have in the company. These types include:

- **Executive director.** These directors are involved in the daily running of the business and are responsible for the decisions they make on day-to-day business.

- **Non-executive director.** These directors are not involved in the daily running of the business. Non-executive directors normally bring an independent perspective to the company decision making and sometimes bring knowledge and expertise from specific fields.

- **Managing director.** These directors are also known as the chief executive officer (CEO). Other directors typically appoint the CEO. The CEO is a type of executive director and is solely responsible for daily decisions and company operations.

- **De facto director.** This person is not an official or validly appointed director but is acting in place of a director. He or she has the same obligations, duties, and liabilities as an official director.

- **Shadow director.** Similar to the de facto director, the shadow director does not have an official title. He or she exercises some degree of control or influence on the board's decisions. The board of directors is accustomed to acting in accordance with this person's instructions or wishes.

The Act also considers the company secretary to be an officer of the company. However, the secretary is not held to the same high standards as the directors listed above, because he or she does not participate in decision making in the same way that directors do.

CHAPTER 2

The Legal Landscape

I t's a legal jungle out there.

Understanding the legal landscape of the corporate jungle is crucial to understanding where your duties as a director fit in. If you don't know much about the basics of law, don't worry. I've got you covered. In this chapter, I explain the legal structure in the context of your duties as a director.

If you feel overwhelmed when you read about the law, know that you are not alone. People from all kinds of professions and disciplines often complain that reading the law is like reading another language. I'm sure you have heard the term *legalese*. I know that sometimes it seems as though it is not even English!

SOURCES OF LAW

You are likely familiar with terms such as *statute, common law, equity,* and *fiduciary duties.* These are what make up the *sources of law.* Basically, these terms describe different types of laws and where the authority to enforce them originates. How is this relevant to you as a director? There is some overlap in the source of the various duties imposed by law on directors.

Many people find the overlap in the sources of the law confusing. The easiest way to understand the legal landscape is to isolate the sources of law and look at each of them under a magnifying glass.

1. **Statute.** A statute is a law that a parliament has made. These are the types of laws most people think of when they think of 'the law'. A statute is normally a written piece of legislation that clearly states what the law is. Both state parliaments and the Federal Parliament in Australia create statutes.

   The main statute that applies to you and your directorial duties is the Act. On the other hand, there are some state laws that apply to directors. For example, each state has its own environmental protection laws, which may differ. I'll talk more about this later.

2. **Common law.** This is also known as case law and judge-made law. Common law is created and developed by judges through court decisions, also known as court judgements. There are directors' duties that are imposed by existing case law. While the Act largely codifies, or overrides, common law, there are instances in which

judges interpret the Act. Sometimes judges will use reasoning from previous cases to help them determine whether there has been a breach of directors' duties.

3. **Equity.** This type of law runs alongside statutes and common law. Many people think of equity as a type of law that promotes 'fairness' and equality. However, equity is much more complex than this.

4. **Fiduciary duties.** These are the laws directors need to be aware of the most. Simply put, fiduciary duties are the legal obligations imposed on directors to ensure they always act in the interests of another person (in this case, the company) and not their own self-interests. It is important to note that there are unique consequences for breaching fiduciary duties. One example is if a director makes a profit from his or her position, another person may claim entitlement to that profit by way of a 'constructive trust'.

OVERLAP BETWEEN SOURCES OF LAW

Are you confused yet? Just in case you're not, let me help you out by explaining how these sources of law overlap. Equity and the common law are collectively known as the general law. While their origins differ, both types of law are legally binding and enforceable. Statute, common law, and equity are interrelated and may work independently of one another or together.

Be aware as you read about your directorial duties that often there will be an overlap of general law and statutory duties. Some common law duties imposed on directors are now covered by statute. In many instances, the statute will simply replicate the common law—that is, the statute says the same thing that the case law says. Other times, the two laws might be a bit different. When there is an inconsistency between common law and statute, the statute will prevail. The importance of this is that there may be different consequences (civil, criminal penalties, and/or remedies available to others) for breaching different directorial duties.

Look in the Appendix for a table that gives you an overview of all of the directors' duties we discuss in this book. The table shows how there are different kinds of duties based on different sources of law.

LEGAL LESSONS

Do you understand:

- from which sources your directorial duties stem?
- the differences between a statute, equity, and the common law?
- the importance of fiduciary duties?
- the overlap between the different sources of law?

CHAPTER 3

Directors' Duties: An Overview

It does not matter how great a person you are, whether you have a good business sense, or how much money you make. If you do not fully understand your directorial obligations, you could lose a whole lot more than just your job. I'm talking about credibility, respect, social standing, and more.

Take my client Mr Rogers, for example. He purchased a fast food franchise, and for a while, everything was going quite well. Cash was flowing, business was good, everybody was happy. Naturally, Mr Rogers decided to open another franchise, where, surely, things would go just as well. His business's expansion continued rapidly—

so much so that the bank became nervous and asked Mr Rogers if he could personally guarantee the company's financial obligations to the bank. Mr Rogers then became personally liable for all the debt the company owed to the bank. However, Mr Rogers's good fortune ran out, and soon he found himself having to personally pay back all the loans the bank had given him after he placed his company into voluntary liquidation. He became bankrupt, which meant, among other things, that he could not enter any more business ventures, as a director, until the bankruptcy ended.

The takeaway here? Only sign a personal guarantee on behalf of your company once you have all the facts, including what you will be liable for in the worst-case scenario.

Practical tips! Keep track of your personal guarantees. Explore options for security you might be able to provide to banks other than personal guarantees.

Know your personal exposure. Say a business-savvy friend of yours approaches you, asking you to become a director in his organisation. 'I promise, you won't have to do anything,' he assures you. 'Just sign here and you'll be a part of this amazing business opportunity.' I cannot stress this enough: *Just say no.* This 'friend' could be roping you into a situation that exposes you to many legal liabilities. You must be aware of your directorial responsibilities. Now that you have a basic understanding of the legal framework—from the previous chapter—it's time to become familiar with some of those legal obligations and responsibilities.

On the other hand, if you're interested in becoming a star on *Today Tonight* or *60 Minutes*, note the following case of my client Mr Sanders.

Mr Sanders was a director (and shareholder) of a major corporation. Mr Nathan served as the general manager. At some point Mr Nathan began to withhold information about the operations of the company. Because he was not confident in the way the business was being operated, Mr Sanders resigned from his directorial position when, in fact, he was aware that:

- The company had not paid a number of employees their superannuation, and he thought Mr Nathan intended to abandon the company without paying those employee entitlements.

- Mr Nathan was benefiting personally via financial gain and using the company cash flow to pay for personal expenses and holidays.

- The company had been trading insolvent for the last 12 months, with client funds being misappropriated.

The lesson? Do your homework before you agree to be a director of a company. Make sure you are well informed about the company and its employees before going into business with them.

Here's a basic overview of some very general things that directors must do regularly. Directors must:

- ensure the company's compliance with the Act

- observe and comply with the company's constitution and its by-laws

- inform the Australian Securities and Investments Commission (ASIC) of any changes that are made to the company
- be an active participant in board meetings
- make decisions for the company and not allow someone else to make them
- seek professional advice when needed
- disclose any material conflicts of interest
- give the interests of the company, its shareholders, and its creditors top priority

The official duties of a director include the following, which I expand on in this chapter:

- the duty to act bona fide (in good faith)
- the duty to not act for an improper purpose
- the duty of case, skill, and diligence
- the duty to avoid conflicts of interest
- the duty to not make improper use of the position
- the duty to not make improper use of information
- the duty to avoid insolvent trading

DUTY TO ACT BONA FIDE (IN GOOD FAITH)

Under the general law, you must act bona fide in directing the business affairs of your company. The Act (s 181) reinforces this. Your duty is to always act in the best interests of your company as a whole—that is, in the interests of the shareholders as a group (after all, they are the owners of the company).

The reason directors have this duty is to ensure they do not arbitrarily or whimsically make decisions on behalf of the company. This requirement protects the corporation itself, shareholders, and creditors. Without it, directors might act in a way that benefits them to the detriment of someone else.

For example, Mr Thompson is the sole director and shareholder of a business called Thompson Construction Supplies Pty Ltd, a construction materials supply company. He is also the company director of Smith Construction Pty Ltd, a construction company that builds industrial structures. Mr Thompson arranges for Thompson Construction Supplies to sell construction materials to Smith Construction at a higher-than-market price. This may seem to be a clever way to bring in some extra revenue, but in the eyes of the law, Mr Thompson is acting in bad faith, as the director of Smith Construction, because he is promoting his own personal interests in his company at the expense of Smith Construction.

It is worthy to note that acting in good faith in a particular transaction may not be enough. You must also have the intention that the transaction will benefit the company as a whole. The act must be *in the interests* of the company.

The tricky thing about this particular duty is that the concept of good faith changes depending on the circumstances. Currently, in Australia, the law on good faith is still developing and therefore unclear. Cases on the subject express a wide range of views, so *watch this space carefully.*

To determine whether you are acting in good faith, take these two aspects into account: (1) your subjective intention to act in the company's best interests and (2) whether a reasonable person would view your actions as being made in good faith.

In other words, you must exercise your discretion in a way *you* honestly consider to be in the best interests of the company at the time. Let's say you chose to enter into a contract with a company, which later turns out to be disadvantageous. If you acted honestly and in the best interests of the company when you entered into that contract, you would have been acting in good faith. What a court considers to be in the interests of the company is not relevant. However, if you enter the contract with an ulterior purpose, this might be considered to be bad faith.

As a director, you have broad discretion to decide which contracts and transactions your company enters into. A court will not be asked to determine the propriety of the contract and substitute its judgement for that of the company. What the court will look at is whether you acted in good faith according to your honest belief that the contract would be beneficial to the company. If you did, you cannot be said to have breached your duty to act bona fide.

The presence or absence of good faith depends on the circumstances of each case. This is why the courts struggle to pin the concept down. There *is* no uniform rule in establishing whether or not, under a set of given circumstances, good faith is present.

When you make a decision and try to determine whether it is in the best interests of the company, take the following into consideration:

- **The shareholders' interests.** Shareholders should be regarded as a collective group. Generally, the group of shareholders is considered to be the owners of the company. However, interestingly, when the company is insolvent (or at risk of becoming insolvent), the interests of creditors prevail. When a company becomes insolvent, the shareholders can't pass resolutions that might have an impact on the rights of creditors.

Practical tip! Keep an eye on your company's financial position, and remember that the interests of any creditors will take priority in the event of insolvency.

- **The object and purpose of the company.** Your actions should be judged in light of the object and purpose for which the company was established. For example, if a company was established to undertake construction of road projects, the act of a director in entering a contract to undertake water distribution may not qualify as within the purpose for which the company was established.

- **Interests of the company.** If you are a sole director and shareholder, your personal interests and those of the company might coincide. However, remember that a company has a personality separate and distinct from the director. More often than not, the interests of the company will differ from your own interests.

What happens when you enter into a contract that breaches your duty of good faith? In these circumstances, a contract is voidable but not against a third party that has no notice of the circumstances constituting the breach of duty. Shareholders have the option to validate such a contract simply by ratifying it with a validly constituted vote.

The case of *Whitehouse v Carlton Hotel Pty Ltd* illustrates how actions done without good faith may be voidable. It also shows that the definition of *good faith* depends on the specific circumstances of each case.

Mr Whitehouse was the permanent governing director of the company, Carlton Hotel Pty Ltd. He had full and complete control of the company's affairs. Therefore, he was obliged to act in the best interests of the company.

His estranged wife and warring children gave him reason to ponder the future control of his company. To prevent half of the voting shares from falling to his former wife and possibly to his daughters upon his death, Mr Whitehouse issued two shares to his sons, which would enable them to maintain the majority of the voting power.

The court decided that the share issue was not done in good faith. The transaction was therefore voidable. Mr Whitehouse had issued the shares to his sons in order to alter the power structure of the company, and his actions were deemed to not be in the best interests of the company.

To act bona fide or in good faith is one of the most important underlying legal concepts. You might hear this term thrown around a lot in the legal world. Simply put, it means to act honestly.

PENALTIES FOR BREACHING THE DUTY OF GOOD FAITH

I give you more detail regarding penalties in chapter 7. But just briefly, here are some of the serious, potential consequences:

- a financial penalty of up to A$200,000 after a declaration of a contravention has been made by the court (s 1317g)

- disqualification from managing a corporation (s 206c)

- an order to compensate for damage caused (s 1317h)

- criminal penalty if reckless or dishonest behaviour exists (s 184)

LEGAL LESSONS

Do you understand:

- the meaning of **good faith**?
- the meaning of **in the interests of the company**?
- the consequences of a **breach of duty**?
- the effect of a breach of duty on **contracts**?

DUTY TO NOT ACT FOR AN IMPROPER PURPOSE

You have a duty, as a director, to act within authority and in the best interests of the company.

When acting as a director, you are acting as an agent for the company; a company needs real people to do things to make it come to life.

Directors are only allowed to act within the express and implied powers granted to them. These powers may be granted by law or by a company constitution and by-laws. The duty to not act for an improper purpose exists to ensure that directors use only the powers granted to them in a way that promotes the interests of the company.

This duty stems from a director's fiduciary duty to the company. One of a director's fiduciary duties is to be loyal to the company in all dealings and to act in the best interests of the company.

Have you ever:

- used your power to issue shares in the company as a way of reallocating the voting power within the company?

- attempted to increase your own voting power within the company?

- used your power to gift the company's property?

- entered into a contract as a way of taking a business opportunity from the company for personal gain?

- voted for and consented to a contract that you know to be outside the purpose of the company?

Hopefully, you answered no to all of these questions. If not, your actions could be invalid. Any act that was provoked by an improper purpose also means that it is voidable, and another person could challenge it at any point.

Before determining whether you have breached this duty, a court will consider several elements.

A POWER WAS GRANTED TO THE DIRECTOR

In addition to promoting the interests of the company, the court will examine the purpose of the power you were granted.

Let's take a look at the case of a director named Mr Anderson. The company granted Mr Anderson the power to issue shares in the company. If the company granted a power or authority to Mr Anderson through the company's constitution or by-laws, Mr Anderson would be acting within the scope of authority provided to him.

On the other hand, if Mr Anderson had not been given such authority, as a director, he would not have the power to issue shares. Doing so would be acting outside the scope of his authority. Directors who act outside the powers granted to them are normally deemed to be acting for an improper purpose.

PURPOSE FOR ACTING

Next, the court considered what Mr Anderson's purpose really was when he used that power. He might have claimed he had been acting for a proper purpose when he issued the shares because he was granted the power to issue shares and he thought it was in the company's best interest to do this. However, it soon came to light that the real reason Mr Anderson wanted to issue more shares is so that he could give them to a company he owned and thus reinforce his control of the company. This is not a proper purpose for his power.

For example, in the case of *Punt v Symons & Co Ltd,* the directors issued new shares to give to additional shareholders in order to secure the passing of a special resolution. The directors were deemed to have abused their powers.

Similarly, in the case of *Howard-Smith v Ampol Petroleum Ltd,* a court decided the directors abused their powers by issuing shares as a way of creating a new majority and defeating the voting power of existing shareholders. This was held to be an improper purpose; the issuing of shares must be exercised in the interests of the company as a whole.

IS THE REAL PURPOSE LAWFUL?

The final determination a court will make is whether the director's purpose in exercising his or her power was a lawful one. For example, issuing shares to dilute shareholder voting power is not a permissible purpose, based on past case law. The director would be found to be in breach of his duty. Generally, when directors issue new shares to control the board or the shareholders or to prevent a takeover, it is deemed an improper purpose. Of course, this will always depend on specific circumstances.

Keep in mind that for the purpose to be improper, it has to be the primary purpose for issuing the shares. In some cases, a director might be acting for both an improper purpose *and* a proper purpose.

To determine whether the director was acting for a proper purpose, the court will ask, 'But for the improper purpose, would you have still acted that way?'

Essentially, if the court does not view the director's act as promoting the interests of the company or achieving the objective for which the company was established, the purpose of the act in question is not proper.

In some cases, the shareholders may ratify an act for an improper purpose. This means that the act would be valid. However, ratification by shareholders will not be an option if the act in question was entered into by the director of an insolvent company in order to prejudice creditors.

Similarly, an act may not be invalidated when a third party has no notice of the circumstances surrounding the breach of duty. If the third party can show that it contracted in good faith, the contract will be binding and operative on the company.

The case of *Mills v Mills* illustrates the tension that can arise when the self-interest of a shareholder or director collides with the good of the company. *Mills v Mills* shows that for directors to act in good faith and for a proper purpose, they do not necessarily need to forgo a benefit that might arise for them.

The dispute in this case was triggered by what could be categorised as a changing-of-the-guard moment in the company's life.

On one side of the dispute was Neilson Mills. He was an ordinary shareholder, managing director, and a company stalwart for many years. Neilson managed the family company with what one judge described as 'conspicuous success'.

On the other side of the dispute was Ainslie Mills. Ainslie was Neilson's nephew and also a preference shareholder, a newly self-appointed director, and a critic. At age 25, Ainslie suddenly came into possession of the majority voting power.

What happened next changed everything. Certain directors of the company passed a resolution resulting in the distribution of extra shares to ordinary shareholders. This created a shift in power away from Ainslie and a return to the original hierarchy, securing the position of Neilson.

The challenge was that the resolution was not passed bona fide in the best interests of the company, because the resolution benefited the directors by increasing the voting rights. However, the court found that the resolution was passed in the best interests of the company and for a proper purpose. Chief Justice Latham explained that to disallow directors to act in a way that is in the best interests of the company but that also benefits them would 'create impossibilities in the administration of companies'. Many directors are also shareholders of the company they direct.

In conclusion, when acting in good faith, directors need not forgo a benefit to themselves, but they do need to act in good faith and for a proper purpose.

PENALTIES FOR BREACH OF DUTY

Under the Act, the following penalties may apply for acting for an improper purpose:

- financial penalty of up to A$200,000 after a declaration has been made (s 1317g)
- disqualification from managing a corporation (s 206c)
- an order to compensate for damage caused (s 1317h)
- criminal penalty for recklessness or dishonesty (s 184)

Practical tip! When making decisions, always consider what the real purpose is, whether it is within your authority and whether it is in the best interests of the company.

LEGAL LESSONS

Do you understand:

- what **express and implied powers** are?
- what it means to **act for a proper purpose**?
- what instances are considered to be an **improper purpose**?
- the general **method a court uses** to determine whether a director has acted for an improper purpose?
- the **but for** test?
- the consequences of a **breach of duty**?

DUTY OF CARE
AND DILIGENCE

Shareholders place their trust and confidence in directors to manage the company. Directors are therefore expected to possess the necessary skills and experience (aided by a general understanding of the business) to perform their role. They are expected to carry out their duties with a degree of care and to not be negligent in managing the company. This is the **duty of care and diligence**.

You can't become the director of a company without giving thought to its running. Fulfilling the duty of care and diligence requires being actively involved in management, participating in decision making, and acting in the best interests of the company.

The duty of care and diligence is both a common law duty and a statutory duty under s 180 of the Act.

Interestingly, I should note that the standard of care and diligence required of you, as a director, may differ depending on the exact position you hold and the type of company you work for. For example, the standard of care differs for non-executive and executive directors. Executive directors are expected to participate in the daily management of the company, while non-executive directors are not involved at this level. The standard may also be different for directors of different types of companies. For example, a director of a small family business has very different duties from a director of a large public corporation. The level of complexity in decision making at a large corporate level necessarily involves different standards and also a larger number of stakeholders; directors are naturally expected to have a higher level of engagement. The way that work is delegated amongst officers and staff is also very different.

You might ask why the standard of care should be different for different companies and directors. The answer is simply that the law recognises that no two companies are the same. This is why the standard of care required of directors varies and depends on different factors.

Does the standard of care depend on the director's knowledge and experience? Historically, directors only needed to exercise the degree of skill that was reasonably expected of anyone with the same knowledge and experience. This was established in an old case from the United Kingdom back in 1925, *Re City Equitable Fire Insurance Co.* When the court handed this decision down, the standard of care required of directors was not very high. A company sued its directors for negligence for failing to prevent and discover fraudulent activities that were orchestrated by one of the managing directors. The fraud caused a financial loss to the company. The judges stated that the directors were only required to be held to the standard of skills, knowledge, and experience that they already possessed, and they didn't need to monitor the affairs of the company regularly. Consequently, they weren't liable for the company's losses, and there was no gross negligence.

However, the standard of care required of directors has risen considerably since those days.

Now, as a director, you have a responsibility to understand the nature of your duties when you accept the offer of a directorship. The precise nature of the duty of care you owe to a company depends on a number of factors, including:

- the nature of the business
- the industry in which the company is engaged
- the size of the company

- the specific and personal experience and skills with which you represented yourself at the time of your appointment

In recent times, the law has recognised that the standard of care for a non-executive director is not as high as that for an executive director. This is because an executive director is involved in the day-to-day running of the business. It follows, then, that an executive director should know more than should a non-executive director. Furthermore, a non-executive director should also be able to rely on the executive director to make sound decisions in the day-to-day running of the company (see the discussions, Reliance on Others and Delegation of Responsibility to Others, in this chapter).

Therefore, the standard you need to adhere to depends on what type of director you are and what sort of company you are directing. However, all directors, whether executive or non-executive, are expected to exercise a minimum level of participation in the company's management. Directors cannot sit back and play an ornamental role; they must be active participants.

A landmark case in the area of this duty occurred in the 1992 case *AWA Ltd v Daniels*.

AWA Ltd was an electronics company. A non-executive director in charge of a certain aspect of the business managed to hide the fact that the business was making significant losses. On two occasions, the third-party auditor employed by the company failed to identify and adequately communicate losses of nearly A$50 million to the board of directors. AWA sued the auditor for negligence. In response, the auditor tried to sue the non-executive directors. He claimed the non-executive directors should be liable for contributory negligence due to the lack of internal controls and bookkeeping within the company. In the end, the court did not find the directors to be negligent. However, the case still raises some important points:

- Non-executive directors are, ordinarily, able to rely on the decisions made by executive directors (see the discussion, Reliance on Others, in this chapter).

- All directors are expected to be involved in their role to some extent. They should understand the company's business and regularly keep themselves informed of the company's financial status and business activities. The role of a director is participatory, not ornamental.

At the very least, as a director, you must:

- know the basics of the company: the operations, the structure, and how it is run

- keep yourself informed of the company's activities and actions

- regularly hold and attend board meetings

- keep yourself familiar with the financial status of the company and investigate further if necessary

- have sufficient experience to undertake your role(s)

PENALTIES FOR BREACH OF DUTY

It's important to recognize that there is no criminal liability applicable to the duty of care and diligence. This duty is civil in nature. Breaching the duty of care and diligence may have the following consequences for directors:

- civil penalty order (s 1317e)

- disqualification from being a director (s 206c)

- an order to compensate for loss (s 1316H)

Whether a director has exercised a reasonable degree of care and diligence 'can only be answered by balancing the foreseeable risk of harm against the potential benefits that could reasonably have been expected to accrue to a company from the conduct in question' (*ASIC v Doyle & Anor*).

DEFENCES IN CASES OF BREACH OF DUTY

Directors can raise the following defences if a breach of the duty of care is alleged:

1. reliance on a decision made by another person

2. delegation of decision-making power to another person

3. application of the business judgment rule

1. RELIANCE ON OTHERS

Decisions made for the company should be informed decisions. Consequences should be carefully considered, and, if needed, professional advice should be sought before the pros and cons of each option are weighed up.

In the event that the complexity of issues involved in making a particular decision requires a director to ask for an expert opinion, he may do so. Asking for an expert opinion is vital when directors lack the competence and necessary knowledge to make a well-informed decision.

But reliance on an expert opinion must be made only if it is proper to do so in the circumstances. It may be inappropriate on the part of the director and a breach of his or her duties if the director 'know(s), has reason to know or should have known' by the exercise of reasonable care and diligence that such opinion is not correct or inaccurate (*ASIC v McDonald*).

When is reliance on others appropriate? The Act (s 189) allows directors to rely in good faith on information or advice given by a person other than a director. A director's reliance on the information or advice is generally assumed to be reasonable unless it can be shown otherwise.

A director might rely on information, or professional or expert advice, from:

- an employee the director reasonably thinks is reliable
- a professional adviser or expert
- another director or officer
- a committee of directors

Reliance on an expert opinion must be made in good faith, after making an independent assessment of that opinion and having regard to the director's knowledge of the corporation (including the complexity of the structure and operations of the company). The director must also consider if it is reasonable to rely on the opinion.

2. DELEGATION OF RESPONSIBILITY TO OTHERS AND THE DUTY TO RETAIN DISCRETION

If a director validly delegates the authority to make certain decisions to a delegate, this is a possible defence of a breach of the duty of care and diligence.

Whether or not it is advisable for a company to enter into a particular transaction with another is left to the best judgment and discretion of the directors. The general rule is that the discretion to pursue a particular business opportunity belongs exclusively to a director. This is the common law duty to retain discretion.

Sometimes, there will be instances in which a director will need to delegate his or her decision-making power to someone else. This is normally the case in large companies where there are many decisions to make, so directors authorise someone else to make decisions for them on certain matters.

The Act allows the directors of a company to delegate any of their powers to others, unless the company's constitution provides otherwise. Their powers may be delegated to:

- a committee of directors
- a director
- an employee of the company
- any other person

Directors are able to defend themselves by arguing that they delegated responsibility to another person. However, this defence will only be available where it is reasonable to rely on the delegate in the surrounding circumstances. If there were a reason for the director to suspect that the person might not be able to take on the task, this defence would not be available.

3. THE BUSINESS JUDGMENT RULE

Not every action that has an adverse effect on the company is necessarily going to arise out of a breach of directorial duties. Therefore, one of the most applicable defences is the business judgment rule defence. The defence originates in case law and is also outlined in s 180(2) of the Act.

The business judgment rule is a principle of law that presumes that directors have met the required standard of care when, in the course of their duties, they make a decision:

- in good faith and for a proper purpose
- with no material personal interest in the subject matter
- informing themselves of the subject matter of the decision
- rationally believing that the decision is made in the best interests of the company

Without any evidence to the contrary, this presumption will stand. This means that a director cannot be liable for a breach of duty just because the outcome of making a certain decision is not favourable to the company. The business judgment rule exists to give directors the confidence and freedom to perform their functions without fear of being unnecessarily subjected to liability. Directors should not be unduly burdened with fear to the point of stagnation, particularly because business decisions are made in real time and often in stressful circumstances with limited information and resources. The business judgment rule exists to reflect the realities of business and enable justifiable risks and entrepreneurial ventures to exist.

How does the rule apply? A business judgment is defined as 'any decision to take or not take action in respect of a matter relevant to the business operations of the corporation'. Importantly, a total lack of consideration of a matter will not bring a director within the scope of this statutory protection; directors must actively use their judgement.

The rule will not apply if the contract entered into by the company is unconscionable, patently illegal, disadvantageous to the company, or oppressive to the rights of the members of the company. It exists to protect genuine decisions made by honest directors.

Let's say a company is engaged in the business of public transport. In order to improve its services to transport passengers, the company decides to buy more vehicles. Torn between two vehicle manufacturers, the director conducts research that suggests passengers are looking for a more luxurious transport and decides to buy vehicles from the manufacturer that has better-quality vehicles but at a slightly higher price. The company does not see the expected return in business from this investment, and it turns out that the other manufacturer's cheaper but less luxurious vehicles would have benefited the business more. The director cannot be said to have breached the duty of care and diligence in the choice of vehicle manufacturer in the absence of bad faith on her part.

LEGAL LESSONS

Do you understand:

- the **standard of care** required of directors in different positions and working in different kinds of companies?

- the instances in which reliance **on another person's opinion** may be sufficient?

- the consequences of a **breach of duty**?

- the **presumption** that a director acts with due care in managing the affairs of the company?

DUTY TO AVOID CONFLICTS OF INTEREST

The phrase *conflict of interest* is one you have probably already heard, but do you know how it applies to you as a director? It is, in fact, crucial to your role. This duty overlaps with many of the other directors' duties I have already discussed.

As a director, you are expected to promote the interests of the company above and apart from your own personal interests. Where a conflict exists between your interests and the interests of the company, it is your responsibility to give preference to the interests of the company. Directors are required to disclose all 'material personal interests' within the requirements of the Act. This duty is underpinned by the qualities of trust, loyalty, and good faith that directors are expected to exercise when they are acting for the company.

To illustrate, I'll tell you the story of Mr Berry, who was the director of a shipping company. Mr Berry was given the responsibility to organise the services of a cleaning company to clean the ships before they set off to sea. It was later revealed that Mr Berry owned the cleaning company he had engaged and was making a profit behind the backs of the other directors. Mr Berry should have disclosed this conflict of interest to the board. Consequently, as a direct result of the breach, the board immediately dismissed Mr Berry from his position.

Conflicts of interest can also arise when a director resigns. Generally, resigning removes any conflict of interest. However, I have heard many stories of directors resigning from their position only to set up a company in direct competition with their old company. Directors who do this may find themselves in trouble. Often, there will be terms in the director's contract that prohibit setting up a competitive company, usually for a certain period of time and within a certain jurisdiction. Furthermore, a director who takes this action may have breached another duty: misuse of information and misuse of position.

The duty to avoid conflicts of interest stems from the following sources of law, which also overlap with one another:

- general law: avoidance of conflicts of interest and making secret profits

- s 182 and 183 of the Act: prohibition of improper use of position and/or information

- s 191 of the Act: disclosure of 'material personal interests'

A company's constitution and by-laws may also specify the procedures to be undertaken when a conflict of interest exists. Directors should always make sure they are aware of these procedures.

What exactly is a conflict of interest? The Act does not contain a specific definition. Broadly speaking, a conflict of interest could exist where a director's personal interests conflict with the interests of the company. This includes both actual and potential conflicts. The possibilities are therefore endless.

Here are just a handful of examples that might arise for you as a director:

- proposing a deal from which you might profit personally

- proposing to contract personally with the company

- sitting on the board of a direct competitor of the company

- using information or your position to take advantage of a business opportunity that you would not otherwise have had access to

As soon as you become aware of a potential conflict of interest, alarm bells should be ringing in your head. Let the board know, and follow the disclosure rules. It is always better to be safe than sorry.

In the case of *South Australia State Bank v Clark*, Mr Clark found himself in a rather awkward position. Mr Clark was the managing director of the State Bank of South Australia. He was also the director and majority shareholder of another company that would indirectly benefit from the repayment of a loan facility from a purchase made by the bank. At the time, the *State Bank of South Australia Act 1983* (s 11) required a director with a direct or indirect pecuniary interest in a proposal before the board to disclose the conflict as soon as that director became aware of the proposal. It also required a director with such an interest to avoid taking part in any board decision or deliberation of a decision regarding the proposal.

Mr Clark failed to disclose his conflict of interest. As a result, he was found to have breached his directorial duties. If Mr Clark had made a timely disclosure of his conflict of interest, the result might have been much different.

The take-home message is that conflicts of interests will inevitably arise during your directorial term. When conflicts of interest do arise, you should handle the matter in a way that does not breach the duty of loyalty you owe to the company. In many cases, disclosure of the conflict of interest will be required.

Although directors must always put the interests of the company before their own personal interests, this does not mean that directors cannot have any personal overlap with the company at all. For example, many directors hold shares in the companies they direct or in related companies.

So what should you do if you find yourself in a situation of conflict? Under s 191 of the Act, you have a duty to notify the other directors when a material personal interest arises. Again, the Act does not specify what a 'material personal interest' is, but it is generally taken to mean a matter of 'some real substance', which has the ability to influence your vote.

Practical tip! Be sure there is a *clear* process for informing the board of conflicts of interest, both at the beginning of meetings and as they arise, if appropriate.

You must give details of the nature and extent of your interest in the matter to the rest of the board and provide all the details to the next directors' meeting as soon as practicable after you become aware of the conflict.

The Act also sets out the circumstances in which directors are not required to disclose their interest, as well as the procedure of disclosure at a directors' meeting.

The duty to avoid conflicts of interest is especially important when it comes to 'self-dealing', which refers to situations in which a director is on both sides of the transaction or contract: as an individual on one side and as a company director on the other. In these circumstances, there is a clear conflict of interest. As an individual, a director would no doubt prefer his or her own interests; it is human nature to be self-interested. However, there are steps that can be taken to ensure the transaction is valid.

For a private company, these steps are set out in s 194 of the Act and may require disclosure to the board (there is a list of interests that do not require disclosure to the board in s 191(2)), and then the interested director may vote on the transaction and be entitled to any benefits he or she may receive from that transaction. In a public company, the restrictions are more stringent but also begin with disclosure to the board. The director is then barred from being present and voting at the meeting where the matter is being considered (although there are some exceptions when the director's interest is of a minor nature).

PENALTIES FOR BREACH OF DUTY

If you violate your duty to avoid conflicts of interest, you may be subject to both civil and criminal liability and further consequences under the general law. It is immaterial whether or not you actually received personal gain or whether the company suffered damage. It is important to properly establish whether there was a conflict of interest when the act, contract, or transaction was entered into.

Penalties under the Act:

- pecuniary penalty of up to A$200,000
- disqualification from managing a company
- compensation for any damage caused
- criminal penalties if recklessness or dishonesty is present

BREACH OF DUTY AND THE EFFECT ON CONTRACTS

A contract entered into in breach of this duty may or may not render the contract voidable. This will be dependent on whether proper notice was given to the other directors of the company as well as whether the contract was ratified by the company's shareholders (if required).

In some instances, a contract entered into in breach of a director's duty may be validated by ratification of shareholders in a regular meeting or through a special meeting called for that specific purpose.

Even if a contract is entered into by a director with a conflict of interest, the contract may still be valid provided that proper notice of the conflict (or potential conflict) has been given to other company directors. This notice is simply by way of *disclosure of the conflict* to the other directors in accordance with s 191(1) of the Act. The disclosure is necessary in order to provide the other directors with an opportunity to judge for themselves if the contract in question may be beneficial to the company. The presence of all of the following will make the contract valid:

1. The presence of the director involved is not necessary to constitute a quorum in a meeting at which the contract in question is approved.

2. The vote of the director involved is not necessary to approve the contract.

3. The contract is reasonable under the circumstances.

4. The contract is within the power of the company to undertake.

The absence of any of the requirements above will render the contract in question voidable. A voidable contract, for legal purposes, is valid until annulled. However, if all the above requirements are present, the director's conflict of interest will be deemed to have been disclosed. The director cannot be held liable even if the contract is not favourable or beneficial to the company.

LEGAL LESSONS

Do you understand:

- the **sources of law** for this duty?
- what a **conflict of interest** is?
- what a **material personal interest** is?
- the general **disclosure requirements**?
- the relationship between **self-dealing directors** and conflicts of interest?
- the consequences for a **breach of duty**?
- the effect that breach of duty has on **contracts**?

DUTY TO NOT MAKE IMPROPER USE OF POSITION

A directorship is a powerful position. Opportunities often arise that may tempt directors to personally gain from their position or gain an advantage for another person.

Under s 182(1) of the Act, directors must not improperly use their position to gain an advantage for themselves or for another person or cause detriment to the company. This is known as the **duty to not make improper use of position.** This duty is similar to conflicts of interest and is related to the fiduciary duties a director owes to the company under equity. It also sits alongside the duty to not make improper use of information obtained through your position (under s 183 of the Act).

In accordance with the complex decision in a case called *R v Byrnes,* what is important is the intent or purpose of the director to gain an advantage or cause detriment to the company. While the specific facts of this case aren't overly interesting or important, what this decision means is that it does not matter if the company does not suffer actual damage or no real benefits flow to a director as a result of a transaction. It is the personal intent of the director that is important.

However, subjective intent to obtain personal advantage or cause detriment to the company is not always required. The court looks to the viewpoint of a 'reasonable person' in the same situation in deciding whether there has been an impropriety. So, even if there was no intent to gain a benefit or cause detriment to the company, the court may still find the position was improperly used.

The judgement in *Forkserve v Jack* dissects and illustrates the fine line that exists between soliciting clients whilst still employed and soliciting clients post-resignation.

Leon Jack was an employee and director of his family company, Forkserve Pty Ltd. He left the company to set up a business of his own, calling it Aussie Forklift Repairs Pty Ltd. His new business was in the same industry as the family business. Leon poached clients and helped himself to business information from the family company for his new company.

Because Leon Jack took it upon himself to contact potential clients while he was still in his original employment, he was held to have misused his position. This would have been the case irrespective of whether he was intending to cause mischief to others or gain personally. His actions were simply not to the standard for a reasonable person in his position. It is important to keep in mind that each case will differ based on what constitutes an improper use of position; misuse of position is highly dependent on the individual facts.

In this case, some of Mr Jack's actions were held to be an improper use of position and others were not. The Supreme Court of New South Wales, speaking through Judge Santow, held that Mr Jack did not improperly use his position by taking a teledex book with him when he left the company and using it to establish his own business. The court reasoned that the company implicitly gave its permission for Mr Jack to take the book with him when he left the company.

However, the court held that Mr Jack breached his fiduciary duty to the company when he sent circular letters to the company's customers before he left his position. The court opined that it is well settled that employees and directors must not solicit customers for a future time when their employment ends and they establish their own business. In contacting a customer *prior* to ceasing work for the company, Leon was 'canvassing' customers of the company in breach of his fiduciary duties. However, the court also opined that once the employment ceases, in the absence of a special stipulation, the employee may canvass the customers of the late employer and may send a circular to every customer.

It may be inferred from the court's decision that Mr Jack would have been held to improperly using his directorial position had it not been for the consent given by the company when he took the teledex book on leaving the company. The timing of the distribution of circular letters is also crucial in determining whether an officer or director has breached his or her fiduciary duty to the company. If the letters are sent after the termination of the officer's or director's employment with the company, there might *not* be a breach of duty. Otherwise, a breach of fiduciary duty to the company may exist.

However, bear in mind that what constitutes an improper use of position will *always* depend on the specific facts and circumstances of each case. The take-home message is that directors are prohibited from using their position to gain an advantage for themselves and must not abuse corporate opportunities.

Practical tips! Protect yourself from breaching your duty to not make improper use of your position by:

- having engagement letters carefully drafted so that directors are aware of what is proprietary information
- being aware of your proprietary knowledge
- being aware of your sphere of influence
- ensuring any opportunity is offered to the company first before personally taking advantage of it and making sure a clear paper trail sets out that the company considered and rejected the opportunity so you are therefore at liberty to take up the opportunity personally
- disclosing all opportunities to your board and/or business partners

PENALTIES FOR BREACH OF DUTY

- pecuniary penalty of up to A$200,000
- disqualification from acting as a director (s 206c)
- order to compensate for loss (s 1317h)
- criminal offence if there is recklessness or dishonesty (s 184)
- Further action may be taken for breach of fiduciary duties.

Related to the duty to not make improper use of position is a common law **duty to not abuse corporate opportunities**. While this is a common law duty, it is important to remember that it has equal standing with the director's statutory duties.

Because of their position, directors may be confronted with an opportunity that rightly belongs to the company and may be tempted to take it for themselves. The common law requires that directors must not abuse corporate opportunities that are presented to them by reason of their office. If a corporate opportunity is presented to the company, directors cannot take advantage of it for their personal interest unless the company decides not to pursue it and has given its express consent to the director.

You may be abusing corporate opportunities by:

- creating a company to take up a contract or business deal from the company

- taking property that belongs to the company (this can include a lease)

- entering into a joint venture or project that the company has been offered (without the company giving you permission to do so)

It doesn't matter that directors who abuse a corporate opportunity are unable to gain from doing so. What is important is that they abuse their position when they abuse corporate opportunities. Thus it does not matter if no profit was received. It was held in the 1967 case of *Regal (Hastings) Ltd v Gulliver* that whether or not the company tends to use or gain from the corporate opportunity is irrelevant. This is one of the best-known cases regarding fiduciary duties.

Regal Hastings was a British company that managed a cinema in Hastings, UK. It had five directors (who, together with the company solicitor, were the defendants) and 20 shareholders. The directors wished to acquire a further two cinemas and decided to create a subsidiary company through which to do this. Regal would then purchase shares in the subsidiary. To complicate matters, at the same time, Regal was considering selling its Hastings cinema and the two soon-to-be-acquired new cinemas. At a board meeting of Regal Hastings and the subsidiary company, it transpired that Regal did not have enough money to purchase all the issued shares in the subsidiary. The remaining shares were then taken up by four of the five directors and the company solicitor, and at the same board meeting a purchase offer for the properties was accepted. The sale resulted in quite a nice profit for the directors who had taken up shares. However, the court found that, through their actions, the directors had breached their fiduciary duties to the company, even though the company could not have bought the two cinemas by itself due to a lack of funds, and the directors' actions enabled it to undertake a profitable sale. The directors were required to account for the profits they had made from the sale back to the company. This case illustrates that it doesn't matter if the outcome for a company is successful or if the results are beneficial or if the directors acted without malice and with the best of intentions. Fiduciary duties are strict, and directors must seek permission from the shareholders for actions that might breach this duty.

Therefore, a director may only take a business opportunity from the company if the company decides not to pursue the opportunity. The director must also notify the board, and the shareholders must give permission for the director to participate in the transaction.

The case of *Green v Bestobell* is an interesting example illustrating that directors should not abuse corporate opportunities. Green was the senior manager of a construction project company called Bestobell. One of Bestobell's corporate clients was embarking on another project that needed the services of a construction company. Green had become aware of this through his position as director of Bestobell, which was going to submit a tender for this job. Green had other ideas, however. He set up his own construction company, called Clara Pty Ltd, and submitted a tender for the construction project, making sure his price was lower than the one Bestobell was going to submit. Green left his position with Bestobell, and Clara Pty Ltd won the contract. Bestobell sued Green personally for breaching his fiduciary duties to Bestobell, and Bestobell won the case. Green had taken a business opportunity that belonged to Bestobell. Green was required to account for the profits he had made from this project.

CONSEQUENCES OF BREACH

Companies can take equitable action against directors who breach their duty. The following might be sought by a company to remedy a director's wrongdoing:

- a constructive trust for specific assets that belong to the company

- an account of profits to divest directors of any gains made by taking up a business opportunity

- compensation for the loss suffered by the company

- an injunction to prevent directors from continuing their improper behaviour

ASSISTING ANOTHER TO MAKE IMPROPER USE OF POSITION

Directors can easily lose sight of the necessary care and diligence that needs to be exercised amongst myriad competing interests.

This was ably illustrated in the case of *ASIC v Doyle*.

The characters in this case are:

- Mr Satterthwaite, a director of Chile Minera

- Mr Mountford, the chairman (also a director) of Chile Minera

- Mr Doyle, who was director of Doyle Capital Partners Pty Ltd (DCP)

DCP was engaged by Chile Minera as a consultant. Mr Doyle became an alternate director for Mr Mountford. Mr Satterthwaite arranged for Mr Doyle to attend a meeting in place of Mr Mountford. At the meeting a resolution was passed to secure the return of some money to DCP that was owed to it by Chile Minera.

The court held that Mr Satterthwaite had failed to exercise the degree of care and diligence that a reasonable person in a like position would exercise in the circumstances. The court also found that he had failed to exercise the same duty when he knowingly helped Mr Doyle make improper use of his position, as it was improper for Mr Doyle to attend a meeting at which a resolution was passed for the purpose of securing the return of money to DCP.

> **LEGAL LESSONS**

Do you understand:

- the sources of the duty?
- what constitutes improper use of position?
- the common law duty to retain discretion?
- the common law duty to not abuse corporate opportunity?
- the consequences of a breach of duty?

DUTY TO NOT MAKE IMPROPER USE OF INFORMATION

As a director, you'll be given the opportunity to read highly sensitive material related to the business operations of the company that often is not accessible to the general public. Your unique position allows you to gain a solid understanding of the status of the company. If you're a fan of gossip, you'll love the fact that you might also be given the opportunity to read juicy material that is related to the business of another company. This places you in a very privileged position and means that you know things about the company that ordinary members of the public do not. Obviously, having access to this information allows you to use your judgement to make informed decisions for the company. It also means you may be tempted to use this information to benefit yourself or people you know. For example, you might want to sell shares in a company you know is not doing very well.

The law has recognised that directors can use information gained from their position for their own personal gain. To address this issue, the **duty to not make improper use of information** was created. This duty exists under both the general law and s 183 of the Act. This duty overlaps with the duty to not make improper use of position and duty to avoid conflicts of interest. Fiduciary duties to act in the best interests of the company and to not make a secret profit are also relevant.

ASIC v Vizard is a well-known 2005 case that illustrates a breach of the duty to not improperly use information. Stephen Vizard, who is among other things a television and radio presenter, was also a non-executive director of the public telecommunications company

Telstra Corporation (Telstra). In short, Vizard used information that he obtained through his position as a director of Telstra to buy (via a third party) shares in three information technology companies in which Telstra had expressed interest. Vizard admitted the breach and was ordered to pay a civil penalty of A$390,000. He was also disqualified from being a company director for ten years. Because of his professional status, the media made much of the case, and this serves as a warning to all directors because it is not the type of publicity that directors of public companies usually want to attract!

THE STATUTORY DUTY

Section 183(1) of the Act provides that those who obtain information because they are, or have been, a director or other officer or employee of a corporation must not improperly use the information to:

- gain a personal advantage
- gain an advantage for someone else
- cause detriment to the corporation

The law has been drafted broadly. It does not matter if the director actually made a profit from the improper use of information. This duty applies to 'other officers' or 'employees' of a corporation, as well as the directors. The duty continues even after the officer or employee of the corporation has left that position.

PENALTIES FOR BREACH OF DUTY

Similar to the other directors' duties we have discussed, penalties for breaching the duty to not improperly use information are serious:

- civil penalty of up to A$200,000

- declaration of a contravention (s 1317e)
- criminal liability if dishonesty can be shown
- compensation for any loss suffered
- disqualification from being a director

The court may also order the director to repay the financial damages, if any, that the company suffered as a result of the director's breach or repay the windfall the director received from the insider trading. This breach of trust is considered very serious in nature, so much so that a director may be barred from holding a directorial post for a period of time and may also be removed from his or her current position.

Practical tips! Protect yourself by:

- being aware of the information you possess and discerning whether it is confidential or otherwise
- obtaining legal advice regarding shares you bought or sold if you think the transaction might have been influenced by information you possess because of your position
- being careful about the information you share with people in whose company you are more relaxed and less circumspect, like family
- having guidelines regarding financial matters

INSIDER TRADING

Insider trading is linked to improper use of information, the difference being that insider trading relates specifically to shares and financial products.

The media throws around the term *insider trading* as a 'sexy' euphemism for white-collar crime. But what is it actually? In the case of John Gay, it was his possession of a report outlining the deteriorating profitability of Gunns Ltd, of which he was chairman. With this report, he sold 3.4 million shares in the company.

Mr Gay was convicted of insider trading, and he conceded that he should have stopped to consider whether the report was inside information. The case is a clear warning for all directors who are considering dealing in financial products within the company to consider what company information they possess and ensure that they have reviewed relevant company policies. The excuse of being unaware that the information was 'inside information' is not sufficient.

In general, insider trading occurs when a director, or someone with whom the director shares proprietary information, uses that information for personal gain by entering into a transaction—for example, buying or selling shares. Insider trading is prohibited under s 1043A(1) of the Act. Examples of 'inside information' include information that is not generally or publicly available that a reasonable person would expect to have a *material effect* on the price or value of financial products.

For the purposes of the Act, the financial products that may be related to inside information include securities, derivatives, interests in a managed investment scheme, superannuation products, or any other products that can be traded on a financial market.

Based on s 1043A(1) of the Act, the person with the inside knowledge is known as the insider.

The insider is prohibited from applying for or entering into an agreement to acquire or dispose of financial products and from procuring another person to apply for, acquire, or dispose of financial products.

PENALTIES FOR BREACH

- criminal liability: A$220,000 pecuniary penalty and/or five years imprisonment
- civil liability: A$200,000 pecuniary penalty or A$1,000,000 for body corporate

- compensating a person for damage resulting from contravention

- compensation for loss of profits

CONFIDENTIAL INFORMATION AND BREACH OF CONFIDENCE

As I have discussed, a directorship is a privileged position. Directors may have access to confidential information through their position that would otherwise not be accessible. This might include commercially valuable information such as the company's trade secrets, client lists, and employees. This is a large and very fuzzy area of the general law. Some information directors obtain cannot be disclosed to other people. Directors cannot take information and use it to benefit themselves, even after they have resigned from their position. The duty to not disclose confidential information is closely related to conflicts of interest and the duty to not make improper use of information in both general law and under the Act.

Directors also need to ensure that company employees are fully aware of the confidential nature of certain information and that it must not be disclosed to anyone else or to the public.

Failure to obey this duty could result in a director being required to account for the profits he or she made and to pay those profits to the company to restore the company's former position, as if the obligation had been fulfilled. Alternatively, a court could declare that a constructive trust exists.

There is no uniform definition of what constitutes confidential information. Whether the information is confidential will vary depending on the type of business or industry the company is engaged in and the specific circumstances in which the information was communicated. Information that is treated as confidential in an accounting firm may not be considered as confidential in a manufacturing company.

There are some types of information we can *assume* might be considered confidential, such as:

- all financial, technical, or business information relating to the company, including trade secrets, research and development test results, marketing or business plans, strategies, forecasts, budgets, and projections

- all commercial, legal, and other advice, correspondence, material, memoranda, opinions, know-how, and information concerning the business or affairs of the company or its related entities

- customer and supplier information

- the existence and contents of any meetings, discussions, negotiations, or agreements with the other company and their respective advisers in relation to the business proposal

- any other information that the company intends to keep confidential according to the nature of its business or as a matter of company practice

The following elements must also be present:

- The owner of the information must believe that its disclosure would be personally detrimental or disadvantageous to others.

- The owner must believe that the information is confidential, secret, and not in the public domain.

- The information must be judged in the light of the usage and practices of the particular industry or trade concerned (British case *Thomas Marshall (Exports) Ltd v Guinle* illustrates this point).

WHEN DOES THE DUTY END?

The duty to maintain confidentiality of information exists even after a director or employee has resigned from the position or company. Obviously, it would be impractical for this duty to exist indefinitely. So when does it cease? The answer is that there is no stipulated period. As with many answers in this book, it will be highly dependent on the specific circumstances of each case.

NON-DISCLOSURE AGREEMENTS

A common business practice to protect confidential information is for companies to have a non-disclosure agreement (NDA) or a confidentiality agreement. This document will normally stipulate a period of time in which directors, officers, and employees are prohibited from disclosing or using confidential information they acquired during their course of employment. This normally applies to disclosing information to another person or to the general public.

Non-disclosure agreements are usually incorporated as part of an employment contract. They could also be signed by the director in a separate document by way of expressed or implied terms. The period during which former employees are prohibited from disclosing information stipulated in the agreement is also found in that document.

The reasonableness of the period imposed under the NDA may vary depending on what the NDA stipulates and the kind of business or industry the company is engaged in. That necessity of protecting the business and interest of the company by not disclosing such information may also be taken into consideration. So even if the director has resigned or been terminated, the duty to not make improper use of confidential information must continue to be strictly observed.

CONSEQUENCES OF A BREACH

Action can be taken under the general law against a person who has misused confidential information or against a third party. This might include action to:

- restrain the use of the information

- return the information or property to its rightful owner

- reimburse for losses the breach of confidence caused

LEGAL LESSONS

Do you understand:

- the statutory basis of the duty?
- the common law duty to not disclose confidential information?
- that the duty may continue after resignation or termination of a director's position?
- the statutory basis of insider trading?
- the elements that must be proved to ascertain insider trading?
- the penalties for a breach of duty?
- what a non-disclosure agreement is?

DUTY TO AVOID INSOLVENT TRADING

Directors have a duty to prevent the company from both **trading while it is insolvent** and **trading in a way that will make it insolvent**. Failure to do so may expose directors to personal liability. This is a very important duty for directors to bear in mind: their personal assets might be at risk, and insolvent trading may expose them to criminal liability.

People who have not been in business for long may think that this is an easy task: Wouldn't it be obvious when the company is insolvent? Actually, this can be trickier than you might think. Some companies regularly flirt with insolvency because of the markets they operate in and their reliance on extraneous circumstances. For example, this is true for businesses trading in commodity prices and foreign exchange.

As a director, you need to be actively aware of, and keep an eye on, your company's finances and cash flow. You also need to monitor the payment of creditors and invoices (like suppliers) and the repayment of loans. If something doesn't look quite right, you need to actively take steps to address the issue of potential insolvency. Do not attempt to keep running the business with the blind hope the issue will disappear.

It may seem deeply unfair that you have to mind someone else's shop as well as your own, but the issue of preference payments raises its head in nearly every insolvency action.

General practice and common sense would suggest that once a company has provided goods and services and received payment in exchange, the matter is completed and it's time to celebrate. However, the case of *Queensland Bacon Pty Ltd v Rees* warns against such casual treatment of debtors. At least a sideways glance is required regarding debtors' solvency.

In this case, payments were made to Queensland Bacon Pty Ltd (Queensland Bacon) by cheques that were initially dishonoured when presented and later honoured by other methods.

The question was whether Queensland Bacon, as the creditor company, should have suspected its debtor's insolvency. In this case the answer was no, but the need to apply vigilance when dealing with debtors was clearly illustrated.

The High Court of Australia opined that any payment made by a debtor to one of its creditors while the debtor is insolvent gives that creditor a preference, priority, or advantage over other creditors. The effect of this is that such payment is void.

It is sufficient for the creditor to merely suspect a debtor's insolvency. A suspicion that something exists is more than a 'mere idle wondering' of whether it exists or not. It needs to be a positive feeling of actual apprehension or mistrust, amounting to a slight opinion, but without sufficient evidence.

In this case, if the directors of Queensland Bacon had suspected their debtor's insolvency and had done nothing about it, they may have been required to pay back the money that they received from the debtor as a preference payment.

The Act (s 588G) sets out the specific requirements and also outlines defences available to a director in breach of this duty.

'REASONABLE GROUNDS' FOR SUSPECTING INSOLVENCY

You should be aware that you can be held personally responsible for debts incurred by your company if it trades whilst it is insolvent. A director might be found to have breached the duty to avoid insolvent trading (as defined by s 588G of the Act) if the following elements are present:

1. The person is a **director.**

2. The company **incurs a debt.**

3. The company is **insolvent** or becomes insolvent.

4. There were **reasonable grounds** for suspecting that the company was/would become insolvent by incurring that debt.

The main issue is determining whether there were 'reasonable grounds' for a director to suspect his company's insolvency. Should the director have known that the company was flirting with insolvency? This will always depend on the facts of each individual case.

Past cases indicate it is not important how directors perceive the circumstances before them. Instead, what is relevant is how a 'reasonable and prudent person' in a similar situation would be expected to perceive the situation. This means that if it would be obvious to anyone filling in for a day in your position that your company might become insolvent, the company might be reasonably said to become insolvent. It doesn't matter that you personally didn't pick up the issue or if you simply say you didn't know.

FAILING TO PREVENT THE COMPANY FROM INCURRING A DEBT (S 588(2))

A director may also be liable for **failing to prevent** the company from incurring a debt that causes it to become insolvent. Again, insolvent trading will exist where a person in a like position would have suspected insolvency.

DISHONESTLY FAILING TO PREVENT THE COMPANY FROM INCURRING A DEBT (S 588(3))

A director may also commit a criminal offence if the failure to prevent the company incurring the debt was dishonest. This means exposure to criminal penalties and, potentially, a stint in prison.

ELEMENTS OF INSOLVENT TRADING

A 'DIRECTOR'

The person involved in the transaction must have been a director of the company at the time for insolvent trading to be relevant.

To ensure that we understand what a company director is, let's revisit s 9 of the Act, which defines a 'director' as:

- a person appointed to the position of a director
- a person appointed to the position of an alternate director and acting in that capacity, regardless of the name given to that position

The key here is that *the person* acts as a director *regardless of the formal title.*

Directors and other people who are closely involved in the decision making of the company should keep in mind that they may be acting as a director without the formal title. You'll recall I explained the concept of shadow/de facto directors in chapter 1.

'INCURS A DEBT'

The definition of 'incurring a debt' is broader than you may think. It goes beyond owing money to someone.

When might a debt be incurred? Below are some of the circumstances in which the Act deems a company to be incurring a debt:

- **Paying dividends.** A debt is incurred when a dividend is paid. Alternatively, a debt is incurred when the dividend is declared if the company has a constitution that provides for declarations.

- **Reducing share capital.** A debt is incurred when the reduction takes effect.

- **Buying back shares even if the agreement does not specify a monetary amount.** A debt is incurred when the buyback agreement is entered into.

- **Redeeming redeemable preference shares that are redeemable at the company's option.** A debt is incurred when the redeemable shares are issued.

- **Financially assisting a person to acquire shares (or units of shares) in the company or a holding company.** A debt is incurred when the agreement to provide the financial assistance is entered into or, if there is no agreement, when the financial assistance is provided.

- **Entering into an uncommercial transaction.** A debt is deemed to be incurred when the transaction is entered into.

Keep in mind that the above list is not exhaustive. A company may be deemed to have incurred a debt under other specific circumstances.

COMPANY IS 'INSOLVENT'

A company is deemed to be insolvent by law if it cannot pay its financial obligations when they become due and payable.

A company may also be presumed to be insolvent if it fails to keep financial records (s 286(1) of the Act) or it fails to retain financial records in relation to a period of seven years (s 286(2) of the Act).

See chapter 4 for more on the duty to maintain financial records.

'REASONABLE GROUNDS' FOR SUSPECTING INSOLVENCY

As stated previously, The High Court of Australia has held that a 'suspicion' that insolvency exists is more than a 'mere idle wondering' whether insolvency exists or not. Suspicion is a positive feeling of actual apprehension. It can even amount to 'a slight opinion but without sufficient evidence'.

RED FLAGS FOR DIRECTORS

Check out the following in your company:

- Company cash flow: Is there a steady stream?

- Company profits: Are they declining?

- Payment of creditors and suppliers: Is the company capable of paying on time?

- Are there any contracts the company is considering entering into?

Practical tips! Protect yourself by:

- frequently creating and checking financial reports—such as balance sheets and profit and loss statements—to check the financial health of the company
- obtaining professional financial advice if you are unsure of how the company is faring

CONSEQUENCES FOR TRADING WHILST INSOLVENT:

- a pecuniary penalty order of up to A$200,000
- disqualification from being a director
- liability to pay the debts personally (s 588M)
- criminal liability (if dishonesty exists)

DEFENCES

There are defences listed under the Act (s 588H) that a director may rely on. The main ones to be aware of are:

- The director had a **reasonable expectation** the company would remain solvent.
- The director **relied on information** given by another person regarding the company's solvency.

- The director took a **break from the management** of the company due to illness or another good reason.

- The director took **all reasonable steps** to prevent the company from incurring the debt.

- The director **followed a course of action** which was reasonably likely of producing a better outcome than the immediate appointment of an administrator or liquidator: Safe Harbour Defence.

In deciding whether all reasonable steps were taken to prevent insolvency, all actions taken by the director are taken into account.

SAFE HARBOUR

In September 2017, the government introduced new 'Safe Harbour' legislation. If the requirements of the legislation are met, the Safe Harbour operates as a defence to insolvent trading.

To rely on the 'safe harbour' defence, directors must develop and pursue one or more courses of action which are reasonably likely to lead to a better outcome than the immediate appointment of an administrator or liquidator.

The safe harbor defence has several elements:

1. **Strategy**. The director/s must prepare a strategy. The strategy must be well considered and thought out. It must be proactive and well documented. Directors should seek advice from qualified professionals. A hope is not a strategy!

2. **Reasonably likely**. The strategy must be reasonably likely of achieving better results. Reasonably likely is defined as

fair, sufficient or worth noting. It can not be fanciful or remote.

3. **Better outcome**. Directors will need to compare two outcomes. The outcome of putting the company into immediate administration or liquidation, compared with the outcome of the strategy or course of action they have prepared.

Importantly, the course of action or strategy does not have to be successful. The definition of "better outcome" has been given broad scope in the legislation, but it is important to note that this new legislation has not yet been tested in the courts. You must seek professional advice and keep thorough records and evidence that your strategy has, or was reasonably likely to lead to a better outcome than the appointment of an administrator.

Safe harbour from personal liability for insolvent trading begins when you start developing your strategy. It ends when you cease to pursue your strategy or, events or new information indicates that it is no longer likely to lead to a better outcome than administration.

The safe harbour defence will NOT apply if:

- There is dishonesty, gross negligence, fraud or criminal activity.

- Directors fail to comply with their ongoing tax reporting obligations.

- Directors fail to meet their employee obligations including superannuation.

- If/when a liquidator is appointed, you fail to fully cooperate with the formal liquidation.

The safe harbour defence allows directors to manage risk, instead of avoiding personal risk at the expense of innovation and company potential. Managing risk does not mean ignoring it, or hoping it will go away! Always make sure you seek professional advice if you believe the company you are managing is in financial difficulty.

Practical tips! Seeking to rely on safe harbour:

- As always, seek advice from qualified professional
- You must continue to meet your tax reporting obligations
- You must continue to meet your employee entitlement obligations, including superannuation
- Regularly asses, review and revise your strategy to ensure it continues to be reasonably likely of a better outcome
- Keep informed about your company's financial position.
- Keep thorough and proper records of your strategy.

LEGAL LESSONS

Do you understand:

- the **statutory basis** of the duty?
- the definition of **director**?
- the circumstances under which the company **incurs a debt** under the Act?
- the legal definition of **insolvent**?
- the meaning of **reasonable grounds** for suspecting insolvency?
- what '**safe harbour**' is?
- what you would need to do to rely on the **safe harbour defence**?
- the **consequences** of a breach of duty?

CHAPTER 4

Financial Reporting Obligations

As a director, you should be aware of and comply with your company's financial reporting obligations.

Under s 85 of the Act, all companies must keep financial records and must prepare financial reports annually. The company's obligation is to complement the power of the government to regulate its financial activities. It is a necessary tool in checking whether the company has been paying the correct taxes and determining the company's financial viability to protect the public against fraud and prevent any scheme perpetrated by the company's officers to the prejudice of the consuming public.

Through ASIC, the government regulates compliance with the financial reporting requirements under the Act.

Generally, according to ASIC's website (http://asic.gov.au), a company has to lodge financial reports if substantial sums of money are involved, if the general public has invested funds with the company, or if the company exists for a charitable purpose and is not intended to make a profit. It must be noted, however, that the specific reporting obligations vary depending on the type of business involved.

FINANCIAL RECORDS

In line with the company's obligation to inform the government of its financial activities of the previous year, the Act mandates that the company keep written financial records that correctly record and explain its transactions, financial position, and performance as well as enable true and fair financial statements to be prepared and audited. Such financial records must be retained for seven years after the transactions covered by the records are completed (s 286 of the Act).

FINANCIAL AND DIRECTORS' REPORTS

A financial and directors' report must be prepared for each financial year by a company (s 292(1) of the Act). However, depending on the consolidated revenue or consolidated gross assets at the end of the financial year, a company may be exempted from preparing a financial and directors' report unless directed by its shareholders with at least 5 percent of the votes or as may be directed by ASIC.

The financial report for a financial year must consist of the financial statements for the year, the notes to the financial statements, and the directors' declaration about the statement and notes (s 295(1) of the Act).

Other obligations also apply under the Act:

- **Obligation to have the financial report audited**. A company must have the financial report for the financial year audited and obtain an auditor's report (s 301(1) of the Act).

- **Lodging annual reports.** A company that has to prepare or obtain a report for a financial year must lodge the report with ASIC (s 319(1) of the Act).

- **Obligation to report to members.** Aside from the company's financial reporting obligations to ASIC, the company has an obligation to report to its members for a financial year by providing the financial report for the year, the directors' report for the year, the auditor's report on the company's financial report, and a concise report for the year (s 314(1) of the Act).

CONSEQUENCES OF NON-COMPLIANCE

Generally, a breach or failure to comply with the financial reporting obligations under the Act will constitute an offence of strict liability (s 286(3) of the Act). For example, the Act provides that the financial records must be retained for seven years after the transactions covered by the records are completed, and failure to do so will constitute an offence of strict liability under Section 6.1 of the *Criminal Code*. Similarly, an offence of strict liability is committed if there is failure to keep written financial records. The criminal liability imposed by the Act through the *Criminal Code* for breaching the financial reporting obligations is independent and separate from whatever liability may be imposed on a director who is found to be remiss in the performance of his or her directorial functions.

LEGAL LESSONS

Do you understand:

- directors' financial reporting obligations under the Act?
- the consequences for failure to comply with these obligations?
- the need to make a note of issues you are unsure of, research them further, and get professional advice on them?

CHAPTER 5

The Personal Liability of Directors

I have already discussed the concept of a company being a separate legal entity. When people are encouraged to become a director or to formalise their business in the structure of a company, this concept is frequently touted as one of the benefits. The separate legal entity acts as a shield, protecting the directors from liability and protecting their personal assets. As with most things legal, there are exceptions to the separate legal entity principle. In certain circumstances, the separate legal entity principle will not apply, and a director may become personally liable for breaches of the law by the company. In this chapter, I discuss instances in which directors of

Australian companies may become personally liable for breaches by the company.

COMPETITION AND CONSUMER ACT 2010

The *Competition and Consumer Act 2010* contains the *Australian Consumer Law*. This national piece of legislation offers protection to consumers and commenced on 1 January 2011. It replaces a host of state, territory, and national laws in one cohesive package.

Section 29 specifically forbids the making of false or misleading representations in respect of supply or possible supply of goods and services. Businesses found breaching this section can be held liable for large financial penalties. Most importantly, a director may be found personally liable under this section. The consequence is that a director could be required to pay penalties, not only for each contravention but also for any legal costs involved in defending the alleged breach. The company is forbidden from indemnifying the director in this situation. This means the company cannot reimburse the director or in any other way protect him or her from personal loss.

In a 2012 case titled *Australian Competition and Consumer Commission v Energy Watch Pty Ltd,* it was held that a director may be held personally liable if the company was engaged in false or misleading representations to the public as to its services. In that case, in a mass-marketed campaign, Energy Watch made six types of false and misleading representations in 80 advertisements across various forms of media. The director did likewise in radio broadcasts in Brisbane.

The court held that Energy Watch and its director, via the radio advertisement, falsely gave the impression that Energy Watch compared energy prices more generally than it actually did. The court imposed a A$65,000 fine on the director personally because of his appearance in the advertisement as the figurehead of the company, thereby giving greater gravitas to the false and misleading content than if the radio advertisements had been spoken by a voice-over actor.

Depending on the circumstances of each case, both criminal and civil penalties may be imposed on the director for breaches of this kind.

There is an occasional but persistent misconception among business and laypeople that agencies such as the Australian Competition and Consumer Commission (ACCC) tend to pursue action against large corporations with deep pockets. Another misconception is that it is only organisations like these that breach their obligations, whether intentionally or otherwise. This is not the case. Equally damaging is the myth that the ACCC will be lenient on small or so-called mum and dad companies. Again, this is not the case.

As an example, in 2013 a small service company run by a single mother was found to have breached the provisions of the Consumer Law. The company misrepresented to its clients their cooling-off rights to refunds in what was deemed to be (as it wasn't classically so) a door-to-door selling situation. The consequences? A A$10,000 penalty had to be paid to the ACCC and an injunction was issued, requiring the company to explain the situation to each affected client and offer a refund on the service purchased. The bottom line is that breaches of the Consumer Law can be a devastating blow to any business, and such breaches can place directors at personal risk.

OCCUPATIONAL HEALTH AND SAFETY (OHS) LAWS

The *Work Health and Safety Act 2011* (Cth) (*WHS Act*) applies in all states and territories regarding the health and safety of workers. This piece of Commonwealth legislation imposes a duty on officers to ensure compliance with the obligation imposed under the *WHS Act*. It is a positive duty imposed on directors and officers of the company to actively exercise due diligence in matters regarding workplace health and safety. Prior to this, the individual responsibility of directors differed in accordance with the varying state and territory legislations. Because a company acts through its officers, claims of breaches of this Act can be made against directors by employees.

The duty to exercise due diligence in workplace health and safety matters is an acknowledgement of the weight and influence that officers carry within a company. It also shows how it permeates the entire organisational structure. To date, the *WHS Act* has been adopted by all states excepting Victoria and Western Australia.

Directors must handle occupational health and safety laws 'so far as is reasonably practicable'. This phrase can be understood as meaning 'what a person is reasonably able to do'. The primary duties imposed on directors and officers are to:

- provide a safe work environment
- maintain safe plant and structures
- provide and maintain safe systems of work
- ensure the safe use and handling and storage of plant, structures, and substances
- provide adequate facilities for the welfare of workers

- provide information, training instructions, and supervision necessary to protect workers from risks to their health and safety

- monitor the health of workers and the conditions at the workplace for the purpose of preventing illness or injury to others

If a director is found to be in breach of workplace health and safety laws, what are the penalties? The penalties that may be imposed on directors who fail to observe their obligation under the *WHS Act* are divided into three categories:

- **Category 1.** A person commits a Category 1 offence if that person has a health and safety duty and, without reasonable excuse, engages in conduct that exposes another individual to whom that duty is owed to a risk of death or serious injury or illness, and that person is reckless as to the risk to an individual of death or serious injury or illness (*WHS Act* s 31). A penalty of A$600,000 or five years' imprisonment or both may be imposed on the erring director.

- **Category 2.** On the other hand, a person commits a Category 2 offence if that person has a health and safety duty and fails to comply with that duty, and the failure exposes an individual to a risk of death or serious injury or illness (*WHS Act* s 32). In this case, a penalty of A$300,000 may be imposed on the director.

- **Category 3.** Lastly, a person commits a Category 3 offence if that person has a health and safety duty and fails to comply with that duty (*WHS Act* s 33). Category 3 has an imposable penalty of A$100,000.

In all states (except Victoria and Western Australia) where a company violates one of the OHS acts, directors will also be deemed to be in breach of the OHS acts unless they are able to satisfy a court otherwise. What this means is that directors who violate one of the OHS acts will automatically be found to be in breach. They would need to satisfy the court either that they could not influence relevant conduct of the company or that they used due diligence to prevent the contravention by the company. Again, breaching *WHS* laws exposes a director to civil or criminal liability. It is important to note that it is not necessary for the company to be prosecuted for a breach or for an incident to have occurred. Non-compliance may be identified by an inspector.

Practical tips! Protect yourself from personal liability by:

- exercising and showing due diligence in fulfilling your roles (demonstrate that obligations are identified and responsibilities allocated)
- having a proper basis for believing that occupational health and safety (OHS) is being properly attended to by appropriate people (reporting, auditing, and accountability) and seek professional advice (if required)
- having an understanding of OHS and information to be able to do this

---

ENVIRONMENTAL PROTECTION LAWS

Environmental protection laws are enacted at the state, not federal, level. Consequently, each state in Australia will adhere to a different regime. Each of these state regimes will impose some kind of personal penalty on directors for environmental offences committed by their company.

However, in 2008 the Council of Australian Governments (a meeting of federal and state governments and state/territory governments to promote policy reform) led reforms to harmonise directors' liability for offences under environmental legislation, pursuant to which state and territory governments introduced legislation to manage the level of liability that directors could be exposed to.

It is therefore important that directors are aware of the environmental requirements of each of the states they operate in. A thorough environmental compliance system should be established for the company.

CORPORATIONS ACT 2001

The Act prohibits insider trading, which is discussed in more detail in Chapter 3. Insider trading may result in civil or criminal liability, and directors can be held personally liable.

AUSTRALIAN TAXATION LAWS

Under the director penalty regime of the Australian Tax Office (ATO), directors may be prosecuted personally for tax offences committed by the company. This personal liability is limited to the obligations of the company to make pay-as-you-go (PAYG) withholding payments and superannuation guarantee payments.

Personal liability is incurred in these instances to reflect the importance of the payments to be made. Naturally, a government is careful to protect its income stream. It is therefore crucial that directors ensure that their company is lodging its tax return and paying tax obligations on time. The personal liability imposed on directors is a penalty equal to the amount owed by the company.

We will not provide an in-depth discussion of the process undertaken by the ATO against liable directors. However, the following points are notable for directors:

- The personal liability imposed on a director will be a penalty equal to the amount owed by the company. Any payment made towards the outstanding debt will be reflected in the penalty amount.

- A director penalty notice will be issued by the ATO to recover the penalty from the director.

- A director penalty is not immediately payable and can be remitted.

- There are benefits to uncovering and reporting to the ATO any liabilities as soon as possible. If a liability is reported within three months of the due date, there are several options available to a director to discharge the penalty.

- However, if the liability was not reported within three months, the only option available to discharge the penalty is payment of the debt.

- In either instance, if no action is taken within 21 days of receiving the notice, the penalty will not have been discharged and the director will be fully liable for payment.

- Directors should engage with the ATO as soon as possible to negotiate the payment of the debt. The ATO is more likely to issue director penalty notices if a director has not engaged with it in an effort to resolve the issue.

It is also worth noting that even if you are no longer a director or are a newly appointed director (where the failure to pay may have occurred prior to your appointment), a director penalty may still apply to you. So if you recently began your tenure as a director in an established company, it is worthwhile checking your ATO compliance.

Several defences against a director penalty notice are available under various laws, which the ATO will consider.

SUPERANNUATION

Payment of superannuation for your employees is one of the most important payments you are obliged to make, and failing to do so can result in severe penalties for directors. The superannuation guarantee charge (SGC) scheme commenced in 1992 and requires employers to pay a set minimum amount of superannuation to their eligible employees.

Company directors have the obligation to ensure that the company meets the SGC. Failure of the company to pay its SGC liability on the due date will make the erring director personally liable for the amount equal to the unpaid amount. A director may also be criminally liable under common law relating to theft and fraud.

LEGAL LESSONS

Do you understand:

- the *Competition and Consumer Act 2010* (Cth)?
- the *WHS Act*?
- environmental protection laws?
- insider trading?
- Australian taxation laws?
- superannuation guarantee liabilities?

CHAPTER 6

Directors' Duties for a Not-for-Profit Organisation

I t is essential to know the duties, obligations, and necessary criteria to create and run a not-for-profit (NFP) organisation. Take the Canberra-based New Connection Church, for example. The Australian Charities and Not-for-Profits Commission revoked the church's charity status in September 2014 because the church failed to provide information regarding the charitable status of the organisation when regulators requested it. This means the church could no longer apply for tax concessions such as exemption and goods and services tax (GST) concessions.

My clients regularly ask me whether their responsibility as an NFP director is in any way different from being the director of a for-profit company. The short answer is yes. The role of director of an NFP organisation is special and often requires the director's ability to be a jack of all trades.

The directors' duties are not exactly the same for each of these types of organisation. The activities undertaken by an NFP organisation do not lend themselves to scrutiny through the same lens used for a for-profit company. The main difference concerns the beneficiaries of the organisation's activities.

WHAT MAKES AN ORGANISATION NOT-FOR-PROFIT?

It really is all in the name. An NFP is an organisation that does not aim to increase shareholder returns or earn profits for its owners. The definition of *not-for-profit* applies while the organisation is operating as well as while it is 'winding up' (closing down).

So simply branding an organisation as not-for-profit does not make it an NFP. There are certain legal requirements that must be complied with for it to be regarded as an NFP. The ATO accepts an organisation as not-for-profit if its constituent or governing documents prevent it from distributing profits or assets for the benefit of particular people, both while it is operating and when it winds up. The documents must contain the essential clauses indicating the not-for-profit character of the organisation. These clauses may include the non-profit and the dissolution clause.

CAN AN NFP MAKE PROFITS?

An NFP organisation is not legally prevented from making a financial profit from its operations. It may still be considered an NFP organisation even if it undertakes activities for the purpose of obtaining financial profits, so long as its governing documents prohibit it from distributing those profits to its members or a particular class of people. In short, stakeholders of an NFP do not receive financial gains in the way stakeholders of a for-profit company do. So long as the profits are obtained within the legal scope of its activities and are used in furtherance of the purpose for which it was created, an organisation may still be considered to be an NFP.

ROLES AND RESPONSIBILITIES OF DIRECTORS OF NFPS

The role and responsibilities of an NFP organisation are usually provided in its constitution or by-laws. The roles and responsibilities of an NFP director depend on the purpose for which the NFP was established.

Generally, an ideal NFP director must actively promote and advocate on behalf of the mission for the organisation. While not essential, it is advisable that an NFP director has a track record of the advocacy that is consistent with the mission and vision of the organisation.

The board of directors is responsible for managing the affairs of the organisation. Their duty lies in promoting the interests of the organisation in accordance with its vision and mission. Generally, the functions of the board of directors include:

- determination of, and safeguarding, the vision, purpose, and values of the organisation
- determination and approval of strategies
- fundraising
- determination and approval of annual budgets
- appointment, performance evaluation, and termination of officers
- management of risk
- determination of legal compliance and financial accountability
- evaluation of activities to ensure they are properly undertaken
- effective communication with stakeholders

CLEARLY DEFINED ROLES

It is absolutely vital for the specific roles and responsibilities of the directors to be clearly outlined and explained in the originating documents of the NFP. This prevents any overlapping of functions among the directors. It may also serve as the directors' guide to proper function as well as a check to ensure that they have not overstepped their scope of authority.

Usually, the roles and responsibilities of directors are specifically stated in the Letter of Appointment, which, normally, sets out the following:

- how the director was nominated/appointed and from what date

- the director's role, responsibilities, and duties

- the term of the director's appointment and any conditions or limits (e.g., tenure under the constitution)

- expectations regarding their role in governance, potential advocacy, fundraising, and any operational or public profile activities

- any induction process (if the NFP is large enough to have one)

IN THE BEST INTERESTS OF THE ORGANISATION

An individual director is bound to act in the best interests of the organisation. The director must have the appropriate skills to make the right decisions and the experience or general understanding of the nature of a directorial function in an NFP.

At the heart of many NFPs are fundraising events that not only ensure continued funding of the programmes run by the organisation but also help to involve members of the community and build interest in the continued welfare of the NFP. The funds raised also aid in promoting the mission of the NFP. Usually, two of the key functions of a director of an NFP are networking and fundraising. The director should have the ability to effectively distribute the workload among the employees, ensuring that there are ongoing fundraising efforts throughout the financial year, as well as various activities bringing the mission of the organisation to the forefront of local communities. A strong director will not merely organise fundraising events but also ensure the financial health of the NFP through effective networking.

The bottom line is that when you become a director of an NFP, you should be clear about the nature and purpose of your organisation and fully understand the expectations the organisation has of you.

LEGAL LESSONS

Do you understand:

- the **definition** of an NFP organisation?
- the **compliance requirements** for an NFP?
- the general **roles and responsibilities** of an NFP director?
- how directing an NFP **might differ** from directing a for-profit organization?

CHAPTER 7

Penalties for Breach of Directors' Duties

J ust in case the importance of knowing your directorial liabilities and responsibilities hasn't sunk in yet, imagine this:

- one or more years in prison
- hundreds of thousands of dollars in fines
- the death of your career and reputation

These are all real-life penalties that directors have faced just in the past few years. In March 2012 the former directors of Australian Capital Reserve Ltd were sentenced to terms of imprisonment to be served by way of an intensive correction order (ICO) following an ASIC investigation. The charges related to false or misleading statements in the company's accounts and prospectus. Two directors, Samuel Pogson and Murray Lapham, were each given two years, and the third director, Steven Martin, was sentenced to one year and four months in prison.

Later that August, a court found that Andrew Alexander Lindberg, former managing director of AWB Ltd (AWB), had breached his duties. The court ordered him to pay a penalty of A$100,000, and he was disqualified from managing corporations until September 2014. The judge accepted that the contraventions did not involve deliberately wrongful acts or dishonesty but concluded that Mr Lindberg had 'failed to perform his duties as a reasonable director or officer would in his situation.'

In December 2012 Stuart Fysh, a former executive vice-president at British Gas, was sentenced to a total of three and a half years in prison for insider trading involving shares in Queensland Gas Company while it was a takeover target of British Gas.

You should keep in mind that there may be additional consequences or statutory penalties for breaching other laws. For example, if you fail in your fiduciary duty, you may be deemed a 'constructive trustee', and action could be taken through contract law for breach of contract or tort law for negligence. There also might be additional statutes that apply specifically to your position and impose strict liability.

WHAT IS THE DIFFERENCE BETWEEN CIVIL AND CRIMINAL PENALTIES?

There are two types of penalty that we have been mentioning. One is criminal and the other civil. Most duties under the Act will have both types of penalty. What is the difference between the two? A criminal penalty is an action taken by the state, with the objective of punishment. Types of criminal penalty might include imprisonment, fines, and a criminal record.

In contrast, a civil penalty is enforced to remedy or 'fix' a wrong. A civil penalty may involve a fine, an order to remedy a loss, and/or disqualification from managing a company for a set period of time.

ASIC may choose to enforce both civil and criminal penalties against a director for a breach of duty.

Criminal liability arises when a director displays intentional dishonesty or 'recklessness' when breaching his or her duties. What this means is that the director displays carelessness or an intention to be fraudulent, deceitful, or corrupt.

Directors may face criminal penalties for breaching the following duties described in various sections of the Act:

- duty to act in good faith, in the best interests of the company (s 184)

- duty to act for a proper purpose (s 184)

- duty to not misuse position or misuse information (s 184)

- duty to avoid related party transactions (s 209 (3))

- duty to avoid insolvent trading (s 588G(3))

Some examples of reckless or dishonest behavior might include:

- making misleading statements to encourage people to buy or sell shares

- participating in market rigging or insider trading to induce people to buy or sell shares

- falsifying records

- failing to prepare accurate company accounts

- continuing to act as a director when disqualified

PENALTIES FOR CRIMINAL OFFENCES UNDER THE ACT

Criminal penalties will vary depending on the seriousness and consequences of the corporate misconduct. They may range from minor to severe. Penalties range from a financial penalty of up to the greater of A$765,000 or three times the benefit gained and up to ten years imprisonment. The director may be personally liable to compensate the company or others for any loss or damage they suffer. In addition, the director may be banned from managing a company in the future.

CIVIL PENALTIES

Civil penalties under the Act are outlined in pt 9.4B of the Act. Many of the duties discussed in this book attract civil penalties, including the duty of care and diligence, the duty of good faith, the duty to not make improper use of position, and the duty to not trade while insolvent.

Keep in mind that the Act is a very large piece of law. There are many other contraventions that might attract civil penalties, but I have focused on the duties we have discussed in this book.

WHAT ARE THE DIFFERENT TYPES OF CIVIL PENALTIES?

A breach of directors' duties may lead to civil penalties such as a declaration of a contravention, a pecuniary penalty order, a compensation order, and a disqualification order. Below, I give more detail on these penalties.

It is important to note that for a civil penalty to be imposed, the contravention must be serious or must materially prejudice the interests of the company, its members, or the company's ability to pay its creditors.

DECLARATION OF A CONTRAVENTION

This is where the court declares that a director has breached a duty. Normally, there has to be a declaration of a contravention before any of the other civil penalties can apply under the Act. A declaration may be made by the court under s 1317E of the Act.

PECUNIARY PENALTY ORDERS

A pecuniary penalty order is the payment of money as a penalty to the Commonwealth. The relevant provision in the Act is s 1317E. A court may order a person to pay a pecuniary penalty of up to A$200,000.

COMPENSATION

Under s 1317 of the Act, a court can order a director to pay compensation for any loss that director has caused. The court order will specify the amount to be paid by the director. Compensation could include profits that would have been earned by the company had it not been for the contravention of the director.

LEGAL LESSONS

Do you understand:

- the **difference between a civil and a criminal penalty**?
- which **criminal penalties** apply under the Act for a breach of duty?
- which **civil penalties** may apply under the Act for a breach of duty and the actions ASIC may take?
- the nature and general application of the **business judgment rule**?

CHAPTER 8

Indemnification and Directors' and Officers' Liability Insurance

Now that you know the risk of exposure that comes from being a director and the potential penalties and damage to your reputation if you are held liable, you are probably wondering how you can protect yourself. Can a company indemnify and take out insurance to protect its directors against potential legal claims?

A company usually provides an indemnity to its directors through formal documentation, known as a deed. The deed is a corporate document that may be embedded in a company's corporate constitution and by-laws or, alternatively, drafted as a separate document.

An indemnity deed can provide significant protection for directors and enable them to offset on to the company certain losses they would otherwise personally incur. It is therefore an extremely useful tool that directors can use to manage the legal risks associated with their role. We encourage new and aspiring directors to explore the extent of indemnity the company is prepared to offer, ideally prior to any appointment.

The scope of an indemnity deed is usually agreed between the director and the company, although this may not always be the case. There are some legal limitations that restrict the extent of indemnity that can be provided, and commonly, companies may also wish to limit the breadth of indemnity provided to directors. From a director's point of view, a deed that provides indemnity to the full extent permitted by law provides the greatest protection and security.

The law imposes numerous legal restrictions on the extent of the indemnity for legal liability that can be provided to directors by a company, namely:

- A company is prohibited under s 199A of the Act from indemnifying a director against a liability owed to the company or related body corporate, pecuniary penalty and compensation orders, or liabilities owed to third parties that did not arise in good faith.

- A company is prohibited under s 229 of the *Competition and Consumer Act 2010* from assuming a liability to pay a pecuniary penalty order.

- Criminal activities cannot be the subject of the indemnity.

Restrictions on indemnification for legal costs are also prohibited under the following circumstances:

- defending or resisting proceedings in which indemnification is prohibited (e.g., such prohibitions exist under the *Australian Consumer Law*)

- defending or resisting criminal proceedings in which the person is found to be guilty

- defending or resisting proceedings brought by ASIC or a liquidator for a court order

The result of an attempt to indemnify an act of the directors that is prohibited by law is that the indemnification will be void and unenforceable. The director would then be personally liable for the loss, and the company could face statutory penalties.

Common issues to address in a deed of indemnity include:

- indemnification against all liabilities possible by law

- agreement to payment of legal costs

- agreement to purchase directors' and officers' liability insurance, both during the term of the appointment and for a period following their retirement

There are also other, more complex issues that individual directors should consider when signing an indemnity deed with the company. These are the issues that will be highly dependent on the type of position the director holds and the type of company. It is recommended that directors periodically review the parameters of the indemnity deed to ensure that it complies with changing legal requirements and, in the case of directors, provides maximum risk protection. Directors should also seek advice when they wish to rely on the indeminity to ensure they pursue the full extent of their entitlements from the company.

DIRECTORS' AND OFFICERS' INSURANCE

Directors' and officers' insurance (D&O) can ensure that the company itself is able to pay for any potential claims that are made against the directors and obtain protection for instances in which indemnity is prohibited. Where claims fall within the terms of policy coverage, the insurer will reimburse the company for liabilities incurred. Most standard D&O policies contain three coverage clauses: A, B, and C.

- **Side A coverage** is the personal coverage of a director when the company is unable to indemnify its director and officers.

- **Side B coverage** reimburses the company when the company has indemnified its directors and officers.

- **Side C coverage** is provided to the company against loss—for example, when the company needs to defend a securities claim as a result of legal action taken by the company's shareholders.

Under s 199B of the Act, a company must not pay, or agree to pay for, the insurance coverage of a person who is or has been a director, in the following three scenarios:

- wilful breach of duty
- breach of s 182 of the Act, which deals with the improper use of position by persons including directors
- breach of s 183 of the Act, which deals with the improper use of information by persons including directors

This provision is a strict liability offence, and penalties are payable by the company in the event of a breach. A further consequence is that the insurance policy may be void and unenforceable to the extent that it contravenes the Act.

WHO IS COVERED BY D&O INSURANCE?

The nuances of coverage under a D&O policy are many and varied. The parties to the policy will need to carefully check the extent and provision of the coverage. It is important to consider the definition of an insured person, as some policies contain a very broad definition of who is entitled to coverage, while others may be more limited in their scope.

It is essential that officers of companies understand:

- who is insured under the policy
- the extent of the risks that are covered by the policy
- which losses are covered by the policy and the adequacy of policy limits
- which policy exclusions the insurer may be able to rely on to deny a claim
- when the insurer will pay out legal defence costs

One reason for the company to take out insurance is to protect itself from being held solely liable for the actions of the director or officer. There may be instances in which sole liability will attach to the company if its director becomes personally liable and insolvent. Thus, it is wise for a company to review its policies to make sure that the company itself is adequately protected in the conduct of its business operations and also to make sure that its directors are well covered.

POLICY EXCLUSIONS

In accordance with industry practice, D&O policies contain exclusions that limit the operation of the policy. The most common exclusions include:

- **Dishonesty exclusion.** Any fraudulent act of a director or officer will void the operation of the policy upon the finding of actual fraud or dishonesty.

- **Insured v insured exclusion**. This excludes claims brought by one insured against another insured covered by the same policy, such as the company taking action against its director. This is to prevent insured persons from taking advantage of the benefits of the insurance.

- **Prior or pending litigation exclusion**. This exclusion will operate to exclude all pending litigation, as well as all claims arising from known facts and circumstances that existed prior to the inception of the policy which may give rise to a claim.

- **Contractual liability exclusion**. This excludes coverage for liabilities that directors have assumed under contract or agreement.

- **Professional indemnity exclusion**. This excludes coverage for claims arising from a breach of professional duty (other than directors' duties).

- **Personal conduct exclusion**. This excludes any deliberately criminal or fraudulent act if a judgement or final adjudication establishes that the act was committed.

'RUN OFF' COVERAGE

A juicy stipulation under D&O liability insurance is to cover past directors or officers of a company. Directors and officers may still be protected under the D&O liability insurance after separating from the company. If 'run-off' coverage is provided in the policy, a director or officer will still be covered against personal claims for a specified period of time. Usually, there is a requirement that the claim must arise as a consequence of wrongful acts that occurred prior to the director's retirement or removal from office and not after separation from the company.

NOTIFICATION

A company and all insureds under the policy must be aware of the importance of notifying the insurer of facts and circumstances that may give rise to a claim.

Usually, D&O policies are written on a 'claims made and notified' basis. This means that the coverage will only apply to claims that are first made and notified to the insurer during the life of the policy and are within the stipulated notification period. Notification must be given to the insurer in order to give the insurer an opportunity to verify the merit of the claim. If this requirement is not fulfilled, the insurer may argue that it ought to be fully or partially released from its obligations under the policy.

There are also instances in which a policy may stipulate that the insured company must make a notification even if no claim might arise. The parties may need to notify the insurer in the event that matters such as the following occur:

- acquisitions by the company in which the value of the acquisition is greater than a certain percentage of the total consolidated gross assets

- a material change in the operations of the business

- a new exchange listing, debt, or equity offering outside the policy thresholds

- a takeover or change of control event

- any claim or incident that could give rise to a claim

The failure of the insured to send notification to the insurer of a relevant event may discharge the insurer from its liability under the D&O policy.

If a company has made a claim under an insurance contract, the company can request that the insurer confirms whether the policy responds. If indemnity under the policy is reserved pending an investigation of the claim, it is open to the insured to request that the insurer act in the insured's interests on a 'reservation of rights' basis pending a final decision.

LEGAL LESSONS

Do you understand:

- the **restrictions** on taking out D&O liability insurance?
- the **importance of notifying** insurance companies of potential claims?
- **common exclusions** to limit the operation of the policy?
- what **run-off** coverage is?

CONCLUSION

I can only imagine that coming to the end of the book must surely feel like coming to the end of a very long and windy journey. It is my hope that the information provided proves illuminating rather than overwhelming.

The aim of this book is to help aspiring and even established directors; it is intended not to discourage but to encourage people through concise, targeted information.

I wanted to show that there is a lot more to becoming a director than people sometimes think, because in my twelve years of experience as a corporate lawyer, I've learned that it's a lot more than people (unfortunately for them) sometimes consider. On the other hand, there are people who get frightened away, imagining that a directorship is a big impenetrable mystery beyond their scope or ability, because they lack a proper explanation and the right guidance. I wanted to help each of them and those in between.

What I would like you to have gained from this book is the confidence to approach your directorial duties with capability and credibility, confident in your ability to comfortably navigate through the corporate jungle with all the duties that attach to the role, aware of what's expected of you and not frightened by the unknown—to have an awareness of what you can handle by yourself and when to get professional assistance, be it legal, financial, or business.

I wish you the best of luck in your journey.

APPENDIX

DIRECTOR'S DUTIES AND EQUIVALENT SOURCE

Type of Duty	Common Law	Statute	Section (the Act)	Criminal Liability (the Act)	Equitable Fiduciary Duty
Acting in good faith/ for a proper purpose	Duty to act bona fide (in good faith) in the interests of the company as a whole	Duty of good faith	S 181 (1)(a)	S 184 (1)(c)	Duty owed to company (Duty to act in good faith, in best interests)
	Duty not to act for improper purpose	Duty not to act for an improper purpose	S 181 (1)(b)	S 184 (1)(d)	-
Care and diligence	Duty of care and diligence	Duty of care and diligence, The application of the business judgment rule	S 180	-	-
Conflicts of interest	Duty to avoid conflicts of interest	Disclosure of material personal interests	S 191–195	S 191 (1A)	No conflict rule
	Duty not to disclose confidential information	Duty not to make improper use of information	S 182, 183	S 184	No profit rule

Use of position	Duty not to abuse corporate opportunities Duty to retain discretion	Duty not to make improper use of position	S 182	S 184	Duty to act for proper purpose
Financial obligations	-	Financial reporting obligations	S 285–318	-	-
		Duty not to trade whilst insolvent	S 588G	S 588G (3A) & (3B)	
		Giving financial benefits to related parties of public companies	S 208–210	S 209 (3)	